ODILE**DECQ**BENOIT**CORNETTE**

Clare Melhuish

CONTENTS

Preface

Frédéric Migayrou

Frédéric Migayrou is Conseiller pour les Arts Plastiques with the French Ministry of Culture in Orléans, France.

Architecture traditionally is an experience of continuity: in planning a project a formal unity is shaped in which the object of architecture becomes almost idealistic. Building is the delicate result of an equation of political, economic and social metaphors, and throughout the process of realizing a work, the building is constantly subjected to rules and regulations, the social and political context of decision-making, and normative and engineering constraints which lead to confusion between functional ideas aimed at the economy of space and the programme itself. When Decq and Cornette define their architectural work, both conceptually and practically, using the notions of movement, mobility and kinetics, they are not adhering to an analytical conception of form, or to a new kind of futurism that displaces the visual point of organization from architectural form. Rather, movement for them is imperative as an element of spatial organization, one that questions the *arche* – the essence of architecture, the very grounds on which the relationship between architecture and space is based, where space is viewed as an infinite domain in which architecture can exist. Decq and Cornette invent an architecture of the inessential, which is almost matter of fact, free from the latest obsessions with metaphysics or phenomenology of form. In their work architecture is succeeded by a real tectonic, a logical process in which the *tekton* enters a new age where the architect is brought into direct confrontation with ever-changing political, technical and legal procedures. Space is thus no longer the precondition to the planning and development of building.

The *tekton* hints at a new meaning of architecture, but one which in fact returns to its historical and traditional – at least etymologically – roots, where there is no distinction between craftsmanship and art. Decq and Cornette grasp the whole range of the project: space is no longer defined in terms of a laid-out plan, an elevation, or something that exists in parts; it is instead a co-extension to elements which find an organization of their own; hence 'form' in Decq and Cornette's terms is substituted by an extensive series of links. The way in which they employ the fold, the plane, transition spaces, layers and the fracture reinforces these as structural events in themselves; they also confirm the link as a principle within the work which, however immaterial, becomes perceptible as structurally important to each work. To take one example, an initial study model for Decq and Cornette's Stationer's in Avenue Franklin D Roosevelt merely revealed the shopfront, a stair and a 'line of tension', literally a curved line on the model to demarcate the stock from the display areas; the effective volume of the shop was therefore denied. Although this may seem to present the architecture in negative terms, it serves as a kind of initial work on the space, which views its own process in time, from its archaeology to its future projection. Another example is a model for their Social Housing, Rue Manin, Paris. This overtly denied the volume of the construction and instead revealed a triangular parcelling of layered facades, indicating a sequence of spaces between public and private in which lay balconies, loggia-like areas and circulation spaces. This exercise on the envelope or skin of the building, initiates a dynamic process, whereby architecture becomes an act, creating and undoing itself in the process of its use. The architects' resistance to form is manifested through their redefinition of the programme; the programme itself is never accepted as a prerequisite to or exterior description of the project. Decq and Cornette create an outline, at a spatial and chronological level, and this provides them with a number of further programmes (analytical exercises on the evolution of the original programme) which, via their interrelation, highlight certain contextually implied postulates.

Furthermore, they avoid the temptation of the modernist tabula rasa or the passive acceptance of complexity inherent in pop assemblages or post-modernist semiology. This is achieved by using the form of a 'diagnosis' which the architects arrive at after cutting into the meaning of the work and which exposes the decision-making behind the project as well as the overall context, the logic of the brief, the precondition of the programme, and the expectation that it is functional. The diagnosis then stands for the ability to apply the raw material of architecture to all the predetermined procedures and decisions in order to radically displace the question of functionalism and arrive at a redefinition of elements that can articulate afresh all the traditional relations of architecture (ie space, function, distribution). The Signal at La Défense is exemplary of the will to reveal this process: this was a cubic structure intended to be reassembled and displayed differently on a daily basis throughout Paris' Architecture Week – a critical object opposed to the monumentality of the Grande Arche.

When Decq and Cornette pursue a diagnosis they implicate the project's components in an order that is no longer defined by spatiality and that imposes a number of operations upon them, which they define as inversion, hypertrophy, displacement, shifting, deformation, fragmentation. Architecture becomes a 'prescription', it intimates a new order for each particular project, giving it its own set of rules. But these rules can also be the work of chance: in the competition for Apple Computer France Headquarters for example, sticks were randomly dropped onto a map of the project's site, and the resulting configuration was used to mark out the services and functions asked for in the brief. In this respect the model is an experimental tool – it

defines a state, and freezes one possible moment for architecture to operate in, but one which is open to revision. The project introduces a method that will be part of the architectural aesthetics, even for buildings which initially appear monolithic. New structures are organically recomposed and conjure up biological images, each structure appearing first of all as a whole rather than as a set of individual features, allowing for a reappraisal of the traditional relationship of space to function.

The elements within the work nevertheless maintain their own autonomy rather than being arranged by spatial requirements. The juxtaposition of vertical planes that are meant to divide the massing of the work, sets up the confrontation of disparate spaces which have to work as a whole. In their Pfaffenberg Project, the separation of the classical facade of the Villa Zottmann, which was to be converted into a Roman archaeological museum, and the distribution of the interior museum spaces developed an assemblage in which the arrangement of volumes emphasized the combination of elements as a whole and as autonomous entities. Their Motorway Viaduct and Operations Centre was a work comprised of two structures: the building is itself fixed beneath a viaduct with a look-out tower emerging through the motorway. The tower and its mast antenna appears to signal a dynamic mobility that spreads throughout the whole infrastructure. The control tower at Bordeaux-Mérignac Airport is another such emerging structure, so tenuously linked to the main building on the ground that the overall structure appears to be levitating.

Architecture in Decq and Cornette's terms is no longer assemblage or montage, rather each work is established by associations, links and tensions which direct the organization of the architecture. Their project for the Centre for Cultural Exchange

in Osaka, the brief of which was to create a visual portrayal of French lifestyle, arranged a spatial sequence of images in vertical planes conceived as slices of French life. Beyond a simple cinematic montage of sequences, the promenade through stages of French culture, along the fractures that organized the Centre, still allowed a unity to be maintained in the work. This aesthetic is taken to extremes in the magnificent facade of the Banque Populaire de l'Ouest Administrative Centre building – a wall of glass stabilized by an external metallic support structure. The notion of the curtain wall has been transgressed by this autonomous object, a screen which both supports and is supported by the structure, an 'ex-tended threshold', as the architects have called it, which blurs the distinction between inside and outside. The spaces can only be defined by their interaction, by architecture finding its original function of organization, linking neighbouring areas. For Decq and Cornette the limit is not a fence, facade, wall or partition; it is, rather, a transferable, mobile space of exchange. In the Banque Populaire the limit is made material by the use of glass which acts as an envelope; the engineering behind the structure seems transparent. The space remains open and mobile; this is a domain whose extension is not geometrically but semantically defined.

Decq and Cornette's architecture proposes a sequential vision, it is dynamically organized, simultaneously material and virtual; this is an architecture of transfer, translation, 'tangential shifts' to quote the architects. Decq and Cornette's architecture of instability succeeds precisely by going beyond the modernist quest for a new spatial definition. In their work, foundation is replaced by prescription, instigating a new order of an architecture based on variation, a *tektogenesis* – a new formation of the tectonic.

Introduction

Odile Decq and Benoît Cornette run a busy office and studio from the top of a rickety old courtyard building on the edge of the ancient and beautiful Marais quarter of Paris. The tranquil, gently subsiding quality of the surroundings is a contrasting backdrop to the intense atmosphere and activity of the studio, and the slick, dynamic refinement of the work itself, which has variously been described as structuralist, suprematist, constructivist, deconstructivist, neo-modern and high tech.

Decq and Cornette have resisted all these attempts to classify their architecture, seemingly unwilling to be affiliated to any particular group of architects either in France or within the global architectural forum where the work has been aired and discussed in magazines and at conferences. Since the beginning of their careers they have made a point of striking out alone, defying the conventional channels of the French architectural system which, like anywhere else, revolves around personal contacts and recommendations, despite the efficacy of the competition system. They have even flouted the conventional dress codes, with their strictly gothic-punk style of personal presentation dating back to the late seventies, which was never particularly popular among architects, let alone in France. This allows them to give focus to their sense of apartness from the mainstream.

As they pass from youthfulness into the middle part of their careers, their built oeuvre is still small, but it has caught the eye of the critics, and created a sense of expectation as to what might come next.

While the structural technology is not actually ground-breaking, the use of materials – mainly metal and glass – and forms – streamlined and dynamic, inspired by aeronautic engineering and the motor industry – is confident and concise, reflecting the energy and precision which Decq and Cornette put into formulating their thoughts about practice and assessing the architectural status quo in France and abroad. Their work has excited observers who see it as a statement of faith in new technology and materials, but infused with an energy and warmth that much conventional 'high-tech' architecture often seems to lack. As one critic has suggested, they seem to represent a first generation of architects for whom new technologies are an accepted part of the world that we live in, available as a resource to other expressive purposes beyond that of simple functionalism.[1] Having matured in the eclectic cultural climate of post-modernism, this is a generation for whom belief in a pure architectural lineage has become an anomaly, while the process of mixing and re-mixing ideas and sources has become a natural one. The individualism of the work produced by such architects is precisely what makes classification elusive, and future development hard to predict.

It was the completion of a pair of new buildings for the Banque Populaire de l'Ouest just outside the town of Rennes, France, in 1990, which brought an international spotlight to bear on Decq and Cornette's three-year-old architectural practice for the first time. The buildings were widely published in architectural magazines around the world, and won no less than ten different awards. The high-tech

1

1 Decq and Cornette's gothic image both subverts and reinforces the French culture of 'le look'.
2 Banque Populaire de l'Ouest, Mongermont, near Rennes, 1988–90, front elevation of the Administrative Centre. The bank brought Decq and Cornette into the international spotlight.

3 Decq and Cornette's admiration for Tatlin's *Corner Counter-Relief*, 1914–15, a dynamic sculpture made of iron and aluminium, suggests a clear empathy with the aesthetic aims of the constructivists.

image sticks in the memory: streamlined metal-clad construction and a dramatic glass facade, appearing merely to have touched down on the site among peacefully grazing cows in the green fields of the Brittany countryside. It is a startling intervention, which effectively satisfies the client's desire to make a strong statement about the nature of the organization. Yet it is also an apposite expression of the process of the city's industrial expansion into a peripheral belt serviced by motorway connections from the centre – an imaginative comment on the character of late twentieth century Rennes and, more generally, the nature of the periphery, or 'edge city', in the recent development of the European urban conglomeration.

Rennes itself, the capital of Brittany, is a town in which the different architectures of several successive centuries, from medieval times up until the present, have successfully evolved to create a well-knit, dynamic physical environment varying between the picturesque, the elegant, and a tougher urban grain. Of course there are some aberrations. But on the whole it is a vigorous architectural mixture, hosting a lively urban life, in which dress, café society, and music, no less than architecture, seem to combine the elegance typical of French culture with the ad hoc improvisation, individual statement, and darker imagination characteristic of Celtic/Anglo-Saxon culture.

Both Odile Decq (b 1955) and Benoît Cornette (b 1953) were brought up in the region and educated in Rennes, where they met in a history of art class. Their adoption of the gothic-punk image which has given them a high visual profile on the architectural circuit, both at home and abroad, reflects their background on the cusp of two cultures in Brittany. The same could be said of their architecture. The Banque Populaire de l'Ouest, or BPO, was once famously described by the architect Francis Soler, reported by critic Philippe Tretiack, as 'too much British'. Its tough structural engineering image is perhaps more closely related to the British architectural tradition, as represented today by the work of Nicholas Grimshaw, Sir Norman Foster and others, than the French. It was the first metal-construction office building to be erected in France, and Decq and Cornette had to go to Britain to examine comparable structures. Indeed, they admit that they feel closer to some currents outside France than those at home. Yet at the same time, the refinement of the image itself is very much part of the French culture of 'le look', which Decq and Cornette themselves epitomize in their personal presentation, despite their apparent disregard of Parisian social convention.

Towards an architectural identity

After the realization of the BPO, Decq and Cornette rapidly became an accepted element of the French architectural establishment, as well as a familiar sight at international conferences in Europe and America. Although so far they have built nothing else on a comparable scale to the bank buildings, they started to appear regularly on competition shortlists. It began to seem that, despite – or because of – their unconventional image and approach, the establishment was prepared not only to accept the fact of their existence, but even to require it, in much the same way as it discovered the then avant-garde talent of the young Jean Nouvel in the early 1980s, and subsequently assimilated it as new blood into the system.

But Decq and Cornette continue to pose difficulties to those who wish to locate them within the triangular structure of the French architectural system, centred on the three poles of Henri Ciriani and the 'purs et durs' modernists at the school of architecture in Belleville; the 'nouveaux modernes' of the school at Tolbiac (also known as the BCBG – 'bon chic bon genre' – or good taste of architecture); or Jean Nouvel and the glass-construction aesthetic of transparency which is identified with his office and has spawned many followers. Decq and Cornette have developed a style of approach not readily associated with any of these central themes of contemporary French architecture, as a result of the freedom which they enjoyed due to the relatively unconventional routes they followed into architecture.

Decq began her architectural studies with two years at the school of architecture in Rennes. The course was experimental in character, placing as much, if not more, emphasis on other disciplines such as photography, painting, video or collage, as on architecture. At the end of two years Decq still had not tackled an architectural project. Fearing that this was not the right course towards becoming an architect, she decided to leave Rennes for Paris and enrolled at UP6, at La Villette, where she studied from 1973 to 1978. UP6 was the most experimental of the new schools of architecture opened in Paris

2

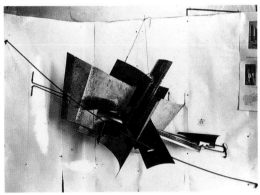

3

after the reorganization of the École des Beaux-Arts, following the student revolution of 1968. It was the only possible option for Decq, unless she was prepared to begin her studies over again at one of the more traditional schools. In 1980 she was followed there by Benoît Cornette, who had graduated in medicine from the University of Rennes in 1978.

During Decq's time at UP6, in the immediate aftermath of 1968, there was a high level of student unrest, and the teaching programme was constantly disrupted by strikes. Most of the staff, including now well-known critics and architects such as Jean-Pierre Le Dantec, Michel Verne, Jean-Pierre Buffi, Roland Castro and Antoine Grumbach, who had been active in the 1968 upheaval, had had no experience of building. This lent the teaching programme a strong theoretical slant. The central debate was the future of the inner city: 'renouveler ou raser' – renovate and renew, or erase and rebuild. For the first time since the war, architects, planners and theorists were beginning to question the need to demolish large parts of the city in order to implement a vision of modernity based on the precepts of the Athens Charter and, more specifically, Le Corbusier's Plan Voisin for Paris. During the 1960s, the demolition and reconstruction with slab and tower blocks of large parts of Montparnasse and the thirteenth arrondissement, and the clearance of a large chunk at the heart of the historic city to make way for the Les Halles shopping complex and the Centre Pompidou cultural centre, had been inspired by this vision. By the end of the decade, the wisdom of such

policies, and the quality of the environment which they had created, was being seriously questioned. When Giscard d'Estaing came to power as President in 1974, he began a process of reversing the planning policies of the last two decades, culminating in the institution of a wholly new ground-use plan for Paris in 1977. The new plan provided for the protection of the fabric of the historic city, and halted large-scale, high-rise developments and destructive road schemes, notably the Left Bank expressway which would have destroyed large swathes of the Latin quarter. It represented a radical break with faith in the modernist vision.

In the resulting climate of uncertainty about the future direction of architecture, and a deeply-felt anguish in the face of the apparently unstoppable pace of technological development, the quest for a regenerative source was directed towards the natural environment and historic urban form as the most important areas of investigation. Among the new Paris architectural schools established after the break-up of the École des Beaux-Arts,[2] UP6 led the way in rejecting modernism and the tabula rasa approach, offering a teaching programme strongly orientated towards typomorphology – the classification of urban form according to typical, historically evolved space and structures, ie 'types' which, its adherents argued, should form the foundation of the new urban design of the future. Decq, who was not convinced by the argument for typomorphology, divided her time between her studies at the school and a part-time job as editorial assistant to the architect Philippe Boudon. Boudon was working on a series of theoretical writings on

the application of structuralist methodology to architecture, in order to establish a framework of laws governing architectural conception.[3] Decq had already gained some familiarity with the material through a course in linguistics and structuralism at the school of architecture in Rennes. But the greatest benefit she derived from the work was a thorough knowledge of Modern Movement architecture – including such key figures as Aalto, Wright and Le Corbusier – which, at that time, the school was not prepared to teach.

As far as Decq was concerned, the typo-morphological approach to design was fundamentally an expression of nostalgia for the past, which rendered architecture subservient to contextual issues and reduced it to a hollow exercise in pastiche. The opponents of typomorphology, including Decq, objected to its precepts on the grounds that it completely overlooked the role played by changing economic and political conditions on the evolution of architectural and urban form. In 1979, having graduated from UP6, Decq enrolled on a course in urban design offered by the Institut d'Études Politiques de Paris, precisely in order to gain a good grounding in the operation of the political, economic and administrative mechanisms underlying urban change and development, as opposed to the technical skills offered by a similar course at the École des Ponts et de Chaussées. The course included a year's obligatory practical experience. By this time Decq, assisted by Cornette, was already running her own practice, working mainly on interior design projects, and she persuaded the

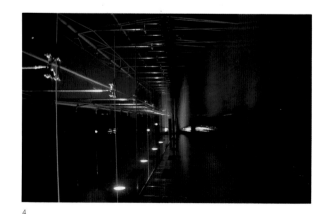

4

5   6

school to recognize this as a valid alternative to working in another architect's office.

In the same year, the French government launched an initiative to improve the quality of public building works, under the supervision of a new Mission Interministrielle pour la Qualité des Constructions Publiques (MIQCP). The aim was to modify the system of building procurement in order to establish an obligatory role for architects in the design of buildings over a certain size. As a first step, grants were awarded to young graduate architects to allow them to travel abroad and study the mechanisms of public building procurement operating in other countries throughout the world. Decq applied for, and won, a grant to Germany, where she discovered the competition system, subsequently to be introduced in France.[4] At the same time, she won a second grant from the Fritz Schumacher Foundation in Hamburg for a research project in urbanism, which she used to gather material for a thesis on the reconstruction of the urban identity, both physical and psychological, of five German cities immediately after the war – Bonn, Hanover, Cologne, Aix-la-Chapelle and Düsseldorf.[5]

In 1980 Benoît Cornette, who had accompanied and collaborated with Decq on her travels in Germany, and worked with her on various interior design projects while still completing his medical degree in Rennes, formally began his architectural training at UP6. In the seven years since Decq had started there, the character of the school had undergone a level of change. Although the staff was much the same as formerly, the teaching

programme had acquired a more practical and less theoretical slant, reflecting the fact that many of the tutors had begun to have some experience of building. The last years of the 1970s had seen the government take dramatic steps towards promoting architecture across the country and opening up opportunities for younger architects, against the backdrop of Giscard d'Estaing's formidable presidential campaign (continued during the next decade by François Mitterrand), to embellish the capital with a series of striking new Grands Projets. The way had been paved by the Programme d' Architecture Nouvelle, otherwise known as PAN, which was established as early as 1971, in order to give exposure to young architects selected through an annual competition. The Albums de la Jeune Architecture, a series of annual publications serving the same purpose, produced by the government and distributed to all public bodies in the country, were established in 1980. In the same year a government circular was published making it obligatory for commissions for public buildings to be awarded on the basis of a competition, as in Germany. It was this step in particular which marked a significant breakthrough in the prospects for younger architects, and made it possible for graduates such as Decq and Cornette to obtain their first commissions at a relatively early age.

In 1986 Odile Decq was selected for publication in the Albums de la Jeune Architecture, with Benoît Cornette, who had graduated from UP6 the previous year, credited as 'assistant on all projects'. During the six years from 1980 the practice, based in Laval from 1979, and formally established in Paris in 1982, had

7

4 The BPO is conceived as a dynamic cinematic sequence of frames through space.
5, 6 View of the mast and general view of the technologically innovative yacht Stars and Stripes, launched in the America Cup of 1988. The mast was an inspiration for the design of the external

staircase at the BPO.
7 Arts Centre at Tours, site Francis Poulenc, invited competition project, 1993.
8 Motorway Operations Centre, Nanterre, 1993–96, distant view of the viaduct and the mast rising above it, forming a symbolic beacon at the gateway to Paris.

6

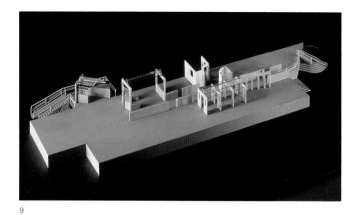

9

9 Crèche at Hôpital Bichat,
Paris, 1984–87 (project)
showing the sequential
organization of interior space.
10 Exhibition Stand for the
National Commission of Historic
Monuments, 1994: a strikingly
modern installation for an
organization dedicated to
preserving the past.

11 The design of the B2 stealth
bomber, characterized by
exaggerated aerodynamicism, is
one of the many technological
references that have shaped
Decq and Cornette's work.
12 Office building for the
CNASEA Headquarters,
Limoges, 1994. The image
reveals the horizontal layering
of the internal space and
vertical circulation.

won or been commended consistently in a succession of competitions, and had realized a number of small-scale architectural projects in addition to a range of interior, furniture and exhibition design (including a report produced for the MIQCP in 1983 on furniture in public buildings in France). Although this area of work was not represented in the album it had provided, and continued to provide, an important laboratory for the development of Decq and Cornette's architectural ideas. In France the design of the external envelope and the interior spaces of a building were traditionally segregated and the responsibility of the architect limited to the former. Hence Decq and Cornette's interior design work, amongst which the most important projects were the Hôpital Bichat crèche, Franklin D Roosevelt stationery shop, Cinéma et Communication headquarters, Apple Computer France office in Nantes and the exhibition stand for the National Commission for Historic Monuments, gave them an unusual opportunity at an early stage to focus on the organization of the internal space of a building. Of particular significance to their later architectural work was the chance it gave them to explore the concept of the entrance into a building – the only point of connection between the external and internal worlds – as an experience of passage between the two via a series of spatial events, rather than a simple step through a building envelope. It also allowed them to carry out their early experiments in the use of structural steel, which they employed for the first time in the Cinéma et Communication project to restructure the space under the roof.

Among the architectural projects the most significant was a new bank building for Crédit Agricole de la Mayenne, in Ambrières-les-Vallées, a commission won in 1983 and completed in 1985. This scheme shows Decq and Cornette searching, less successfully at this stage, for a mode of expression in the external envelope of the building. The rather mannered, symmetrical entrance facade, crowned by a glazed barrel vault between a pair of gable ends, clearly shows the influence of the debate surrounding the search for a new architectural syntax, which was at that time at its height. Decq described it as a 'transplant operation', or a 'play of antagonisms' between an idea of modernity and the historic vernacular and local customs of the small rural town in which it is situated.[6] These ideas were to be developed in subsequent work, though the architectural language itself was to change almost beyond recognition.

By the mid-eighties Decq and Cornette had established themselves as architects on their own account with considerable experience of the construction process, through their first-hand involvement with small interior design projects, but in the unusual position of never having worked for anyone else. Whereas most young graduating architects passed from college to the office of an established practice for at least a period of apprenticeship, Decq and Cornette struck out on their own from the outset. This gave them a rare freedom from the influence of imposed ideas about either methodology or approach, but at the same time it deprived them of the benefits to be gained from working with more mature designers on larger-

10

11

12

scale projects. Their early initiation into the rites of the building site meant that they had little time to work out a theoretical position of their own independently of the practical demands imposed by the construction process. Hence their architectural philosophy was to develop gradually during the work, project by project in a rather ad hoc way, as a mixture of experimentation and theory determined to a large degree by practical experience, rather than ideology or dogma. As a result some of the earlier architectural work has a raw, unformed quality about it, but, on the other hand, the absence of any ideological or methodological straitjacket allows a certain freshness and spontaneity to come through.

In this respect, there is a contrast between the work that they have produced, and much contemporary French architecture with its underlying tendency towards ideological statement, and antipathy to the jokey or critical irony which underlies contemporary post-modern, or 'pop' architecture in, say, Britain, the United States or Japan. This tendency has been largely generated by the system of political patronage which has itself stimulated the production of so much new architecture in the last decade. In particular, there has emerged a whole generation of glass buildings inspired by the idea of expressing a concept of the transparency, or visibility, of the democratic political process, as well as making a dramatic visual statement about the political prestige of the client. The emphasis placed on the external image of a building has firm roots in the Beaux-Arts tradition, which remains very strong in France, and was

furthermore enforced by the traditional construction contract by which the architect assumed responsibility only for the building envelope. More recently, the introduction of the competition system, and the pressure it exerted on architects to produce an identity sufficiently striking to impress a jury, heightened still further the importance of the building image.

Decq and Cornette have stated that the concept of transparency is one in which they are not at all interested. On the other hand, as part of that generation of architects reaching forty years old which has benefited, or hoped to, from the introduction of the competition system, they have necessarily been responsive to the need for a certain quality of architectural image. In the case of the BPO, it was to a great extent the glass facade which caught the imagination of the client, the critics and the public. But Decq and Cornette insisted that this crucial element of the design was conceived in the first place as a means of allowing people working inside the building to see out onto, and relate to, the surrounding countryside, and only secondarily as a strong, forward-looking image that would reflect the aspirations of the client organization and the way in which it wished to present itself to the public.

Central to Decq and Cornette's architectural approach is the belief that a building cannot be reduced to a single image. The Beaux-Arts tradition, with its emphasis on symmetry and *parti*, generated a static architecture designed to be understood as a single grand idea. By contrast, it is the Modern Movement concept of architecture as a series of

spatial sequences, or 'parcours' (promenade), which constitutes the strong organizing principle in Decq and Cornette's work, and can be seen as a natural development from their early experience designing interior spaces, as opposed to building envelopes. Although they have emphasized that buildings cannot be equated with cinema as such, they themselves draw parallels between the narrative structure of film, and the way they develop their architectural ideas as a succession of cuts revealing space from different angles, in contrast to the all-embracing vista of the Beaux-Arts model. They particularly admire the work of contemporary film-makers such as Quentin Tarantino or Oliver Stone who, in his controversial production *Natural Born Killers*, exploited techniques including collage and animation in order to manipulate conventional narrative structure; while there are also similarities between the slick, polished surfaces and pop, cult status of Tarantino's films, and the projects of Decq and Cornette, with their strong visual and slightly anti-establishment appeal.

'L'équilibre dynamique' (dynamic equilibrium) is the term which Decq and Cornette have turned into common currency in their office to capture the sense of this idea of constant movement, generating balance and stability, which underlies their work. But it expresses an attitude, rather than a set of rules: a broad perception of the modern condition and its reflection in architecture, which they summed up in the project 'Hyper-Tension', for the exhibition 'Application et Implication: modèle de penser, acte de présence' at the Centre National d'Art Contemporain, Grenoble, in 1993. They wrote:

'If modernity, in the sense defined by Baudelaire, is "the transitory, the fugitive, the contingent", then the essential attribute of modernity is movement.

'Today, in the face of the apparently sudden collapse ... of established systems which everyone thought were eternal, the architect, like everyone else, is caught up in a whirlwind ... which nobody seems able to control ... Doubt, confusion, anxiety and loss of confidence in his own role are the dominant sentiments.

'During our time as architects we have often been led to feel at the limits of a situation. To be on the edge of a precipice, two steps from breaking-point or from collapse, is the essence of this condition of total instability.

'Confronted by this more-or-less permanent sensation, we have always thought that to be in a state of movement, to move, and thus to go forward, would allow us to preserve our balance.' [7]

The Hyper-Tension installation demonstrated the essential generative elements of such an architecture: 'The variety of lines of force [lignes de fuite] and perspective generates a permanent tension ... The parcours ... ensures a sequential perception of the space ... The threshold itself is extended, so that the boundary between interior and exterior becomes ambiguous.'[8] Some years before, in autumn 1989, Decq and Cornette had exhibited a series of coloured architectural models, entitled 'Maquettes Invraisemblables [Unrealistic Models]: "The Model is the Message"', which demonstrated the same principles on a smaller scale. The models, relating to a series of projects, were working tools produced not to illustrate in a realistic manner the intended form and appearance of the building, but to communicate the essential design ideas involved in each case, using colour as a coding system for materials and structural elements. In his catalogue essay, the critic Martin Mead commented: ' ... even in the surprising, almost caricatural, case of one of the models for the rue Manin flats, where the structural wall planes are deformed in exaggerated optical perspective, it nevertheless succeeds in its intended objective of imaginatively conveying [the] dynamic, kinetic vision one would experience when walking towards and through the building in reality'.[9] Decq's former employer and colleague Philippe Boudon wrote: 'By comparison with the freedom of expression, the heuristic possibilities that an architect is able to explore in his drawings of a scheme, the scale model, more often than not, presents such a realistic image that it fails to capture the same degree of interest. The models dealt with here are however of quite a different order, for they are what can be termed FIGURES OF ARCHITECTURAL CONCEPTION.' [10]

Decq and Cornette's models play an essential role in the process of developing, as well as communicating, a fundamentally physical and pragmatic concept of architecture based on sequential operations, contrasts and dissociation between elements, project by project, which they believe reflects the complexity of the modern condition. Coloured study models are constructed for the purpose of experimentation and research, using free-floating elements which can be moved around quickly and freely. The next stage comprises testing or verification, and the fixing of a design, while the final stage is the production of the pure white model, precisely constructed, for competition submission. Conceptual continuity is established through a process of analysing each project after it is completed, and developing the ideas in the next, even using and adapting a model in a subsequent project. But Decq and Cornette insist that no project is ever approached with a preconceived framework of ideas. Each is addressed on its own terms, as a unique combination of programmatic, constructional, and contextual requirements, in a process of analysis, followed by proposed treatment, which Cornette has compared to that of medical diagnosis and prescription.

This is architecture conceived as process, rather than image or monument. The approach extends to the occupation of the site and the way in which context is addressed. Decq and Cornette use a technique of site analysis which involves tracing grids and 'lines of force' across a terrain to form a compositional framework, demonstrated with particular clarity in their Airlande and Port de Gennevilliers schemes. This generates a deep sense or logic determining the situation of buildings on the ground. The relationships between them are governed by the same ideas as the relationship of parts to the whole within a single building: dynamic tension between straight and curved lines, 'parcours' or promenade, physical and visual connection or dissociation of elements, variety of perspective, and association of functions. These constitute the founding principles of Decq and Cornette's urban approach, equally applicable to the historic city or the periphery, with which they challenge the

13 Hyper-Tension installation, Grenoble, 1993, designed to illustrate the architectural principles behind the work.
14 'Clara-Clara' by sculptor Richard Serra, 1983 (here shown in the Jardin des Tuileries, Paris) illustrates a dynamic tension in its curved lines.
15 Model of the BPO showing geometry generating the site layout.

14

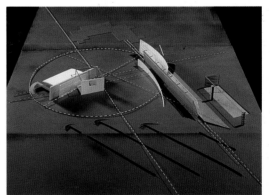

15

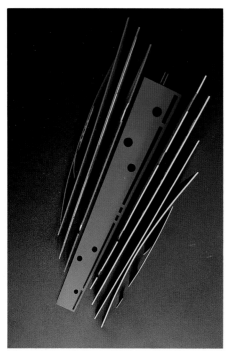

16

16 Social housing at rue Manin, Paris, 1987–89. The model highlights the architects' concept of a layered facade.
17 Centre for Cultural Exchange, Osaka, 1991. The model developed out of the rue Manin model and extended the concept of layering through

the whole volume of the proposed building.
18 Airlande Business Park proposal, Rennes, 1992. The plan shows superimposed grids traced across the site as the basis for the layout's development.

rationale of current planning policy based on purely visual criteria. In Paris, as in other historic cities all over the world, planning policy became increasingly restrictive during the 1980s and preservation became a priority. Conservation areas were established in which, where new building was permitted at all, architects were subjected to pressure to build behind existing facades, or to copy the original architecture. Outside those areas, architects were obliged to work within strict development masterplans governing density, volume, scale, materials and even architectural style. Decq and Cornette first confronted these issues with their rue Manin housing project in Paris' nineteenth arrondissement, masterplanned by Alain Sarfati. Although there was no obligation to build in a historic style, what they could and could not do was strictly controlled, with the result that the building is scarcely distinguishable from its neighbours, although the design of the facade as a three-dimensional series of layers was taken to the furthest possible limits.

Decq and Cornette believe that the integration of new buildings into the historic fabric cannot be achieved through simple mimeticism, but rather through forging other, more profound relationships between the new and the old. Difference, they argue, complements historic buildings better than pastiche. The real issue is to tackle the question of the organization of functions in the city of tomorrow. This requires a serious discussion about the future of the city which acknowledges the significance and value of discontinuity, as opposed to continuity, in its development. With the 1994 commission to design

the masterplan for the revitalization of the docks at the Port de Gennevilliers in Paris – their first urban masterplan – Decq and Cornette were finally being given the opportunity to make a substantial contribution to this discussion in real architectural terms. Their scheme is based on the principle of mixed development, taking historic infrastructure and use patterns as the starting point for the construction of a new development grid appropriate to contemporary conditions and needs.

In pursuit of dynamic equilibrium
The problem or, otherwise viewed, the challenge posed by an architecture of movement and discontinuity, as opposed to traditional architectural values of solidity, anchoring and continuity, is a level of complexity which necessitates a very high degree of precision in the construction, and also potentially high costs. The shape of Decq and Cornette's architecture developed very closely in relationship to their experience, early on, of the construction process and the realities of the site, albeit on a small scale. They quickly understood that they could not realize the architecture of their imagination in concrete, the preferred building material of the French construction industry. Indeed, it would have been impossible to execute their designs in concrete with the structural precision required, both because of the nature of the material, and because of the relatively low quality of craftsmanship available in France and the nature of the French construction contract, which gives the contractor greater control than the architect over detailing. Besides, concrete was simply too static a material to

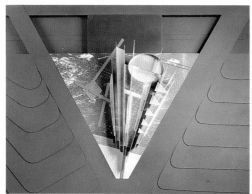

17

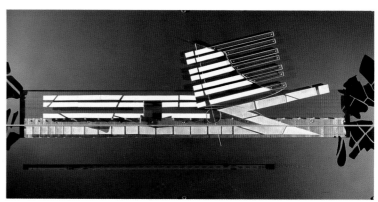

18

give expression to the idea of movement driving the architectural conception. It was these considerations – heightened, Cornette believes, by the influence of his scientific training, which had impressed upon him the importance of precision and accuracy – rather than any a priori preference for metal over concrete that led Decq and Cornette to pursue the possibility of building in metal, despite the dearth of French engineers (with the notable exception of Marc Mimram) skilled and experienced in this area of construction technology, and the lack of French examples of metal buildings. By comparison, British expertise, represented in France during this period by the firm of Rice Francis Ritchie, headed by Peter Rice, was very much greater, and British contemporary architecture offered an impressive array of examples of metal construction designed by internationally known architects. Decq and Cornette, already enamoured of British rock music and street style, thus developed an increasingly strong interest in current British architecture, in which they recognized a concept of assemblage – as opposed to the French ideals of anchored mass, or weightless transparency – for which they felt a deep affinity.

Yet the accusation, levelled by Soler, of being 'too much British' in their outlook and approach is hardly a balanced view. Metal and glass construction is not, after all, unique to Britain, but common to all the industrialized countries. France has its own tradition of industrial construction in metal and glass (represented most ostentatiously by the construction of the Eiffel Tower) – almost as long as the British, dating back to the later eighteenth

century and culminating in the work of Prouvé and Chareau. Decq and Cornette acknowledge the inspiration of the latter, but are altogether less interested in identifying any specific spiritual ancestors, be they French or British, than in establishing themselves as part of a general and universal historical process by which the quantity of materials used in construction has been consistently pared away to the minimum attainable by the technology of any given time.

The reluctance to acknowledge any direct influences or affiliations, whether they be persons or theories, historical or contemporary, is noticeable in Decq and Cornette's own view of their work, and perhaps exaggerates the impression of their isolation, or independence, in French and international architectural thought and practice. The relationships which have been most important to them in developing their ideas and attitude have not been with other architects, but with critics, academics and artists with whom they have forged close friendships. These people include Philippe Boudon and Michel Vernes from their student days; the Paris-based English historian and critic Martin Mead, and Richard Edwards, director of the Fondation Ledoux at Arc et Senans, who introduced them to Paul Virilio in the late eighties; Philippe Tretiack, architect and critic for the magazine *D'Architecture*; and, more recently, Frédéric Migayrou, secretary of the Fondation Régional d'Art Contemporain; the German art historian and architectural critic Andreas Ruby; Melvin Charney, the Canadian architect and artist; and Yehuda Safran, philosopher and former

teacher at the Architectural Association in London; plus, of course, the late Peter Rice and his collaborator at RFR, Hugh Dutton.

While Decq and Cornette's detachment is partly a form of conscious resistance to the process of categorization by critics which can often distort the debate in contemporary architecture, it is also representative of the influence exerted by the broad movement towards eclecticism which developed internationally during the seventies and eighties as a result of the re-evaluation of the Modern Movement throughout Europe and America. Like many contemporary architects Decq and Cornette have rejected the architectural rules or dogma of modernism, drawing on many and varied sources external to architecture in its place, while supporting the more general idea of progress and the social and cultural vision which lay at its core. They embrace the idea of functional performance as a fundamental basis for architecture, in the same way as it is the basis for the production of any industrial object, but reject the tyranny of functionalism in favour of freedom of functional expression. Their relationship to the emergent new mainstreams of architectural thought shaping practice during the period concerned is equally loose. In the early work there are clearly reflections of the post-modernist discourse around the search for a new language of architecture, while the later work, including the BPO, bears witness to the influence of deconstruction. Decq and Cornette do not acknowledge any direct influence from either school of thought, but both offered a freedom which clearly appealed to them – post-modernism in its

19

20

Decq and Cornette locate their work within a tradition of sophisticated architectural engineering which, in the nineteenth century, was no less developed in France than it was in England; French architects of the twentieth century such as Prouvé and Chareau have had an enduring influence on successive generations up to the present day.
19 Pierre Chareau's Maison de Verre, Paris, 1931, view of staircase.
20 Panel for an aluminium shed roof designed by Henri Prouvé, with Jean Prouvé consulting.
21 Drawing by Claude Prouvé for the CNIT building at La Défense, 1956.

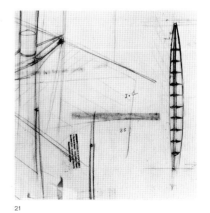

21

22

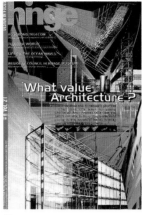

23

24

critical irony and humour, deconstruction in the legitimacy it gave to the concept of dissociation of elements. However Decq and Cornette themselves have preferred to emphasize the role of inspiration derived from areas of cultural production external to the immediate architectural debate, particularly cinema and contemporary art. Donald Judd's empty boxes, Richard Serra's metal constructions, and Robert Irwin's explorations of light, space and colour figure large among the work for which they feel a strong affinity. But there is also a more general sense in which they aspire to the freedom of research and experimentation enjoyed by the artist and conventionally denied to the architect by economic constraints. Decq and Cornette's model-making activity, as an expressive vehicle for ideas rather than for the realistic representation of built form, occupies an ambiguous middle-ground between the processes of architecture and art. They believe there is a need to strengthen the connections between architecture and art, although they have so far felt unable to develop any real projects in collaboration with artists because of the way in which the one per cent for art system in France has operated to promote an emphasis on the production of art objects rather than the exploration of interaction between space and light.

Apart from cinema and art, technology has clearly had a profound influence on Decq and Cornette's architectural imagination. They have a great love for the imagery of industrially-produced objects, such as cars, boats, and aeroplanes, associated with speed, movement and balance. By contrast, they have an undisguised aversion to the imagery of the

natural and organic, or at least until it has been subjected to some kind of intellectual transformation. On the other hand, they are committed to the development of a more environmentally-friendly, sustainable architecture through research into, and development of, industrial production techniques. It is this line of enquiry, rather than a return to organicism in architecture, which they believe holds the key to the production of high-performance buildings minimizing environmental damage. As Paul Virilio put it: 'We are no longer dealing with the technology of construction but with the construction of technology.'[11]

Although Decq and Cornette have gained an international profile as much by their presence on the international conference circuit as by their architectural production, they have played down the role of theory in their work, always emphasizing that their theoretical positions, such as they exist, have developed through, and as a result of, practice. This is partly due to the fact of having studied at a school which did not teach any particular line of architectural doctrine, so that they never acquired the habit of working within the parameters of predetermined rules and solutions. The core of their philosophy as it has evolved since then is the concept of a process of continuous research into the idea of balance and stability within a state of continuous movement. Hence the work does not occur within a conceptual vacuum, rather it is shaped through a process of gradual development and transformation, underpinned by an open attitude towards experimentation which embraces the idea of occasionally doing projects 'contre la nature'

('against their nature'), rather than any given system of rules. Decq and Cornette's explanation is that: 'any system of [static] thought which presents itself as absolute and definitive, such as, for example, the Modern Movement (insofar as some have wished to reduce it to an order and a doctrine) becomes incapable of responding to the complexity of our environment.'[12] This is the difference, they argue, between theory and doctrine. Theory is 'an attitude of dissatisfaction, of doubt, which leads one to reject the established order or conventions. To think in terms of theory is to make a proposition which one accepts at the outset may be called into question ... to entertain doubt and subject to criticism is the principle and foundation of the scientific process'. By contrast, 'to think in terms of doctrine is usually to sterilize thought and thus creativity by dogma, certainty of the truth, and the need for a priori belief'.[13] While they object to the latter, they favour the former, tested and verified through experimentation, believing that 'the starting-point of the process of architectural conception is in intellectual speculation and the field of ideas.' [14]

The great hindrance to architectural experimentation in France is, ironically, the dearth of small-scale, privately-funded projects. While French architects have benefited enormously from a system of architectural patronage and building procurement which has made public building commissions peculiarly accessible to relatively young practitioners, the lack of private house-building commissions has deprived those same individuals of the opportunity to explore ideas in the way that has, for example, been seen in the United States, making it an important

25   26

22   Catalogue booklet to the
exhibition 'Maquettes
Invraisemblables: The Model is
the Message', in which Decq
and Cornette highlighted
the role of the model in the
design process.
23, 24   Magazine covers
featuring Decq and Cornette's
work bear witness to their
international media profile.
25, 26   Odile Decq and Benoît
Cornette participate in the
Academy Group's 'Pop
Architecture' and 'Theory and
Experimentation' Symposia at
the Royal Academy of Arts,
London, November 1991, and
June 1992, respectively.
27   Bordeaux-Mérignac
Airport, Control Tower and
Technical Building, 1993, an
exaggerated contrast of vertical
and horizontal elements.

seedbed for new developments. Decq and Cornette believe this to be a serious problem, exacerbating the wider malaise of a national culture which they regard as introverted and unwilling to know about or acknowledge cultural developments taking place beyond its own borders. Their own response has been to make a concerted effort to forge their own links with developments abroad. Since Decq's first grant-funded study trip to Germany, both she and Cornette have regularly travelled abroad to attend conferences and exhibit their work, while in 1987 they produced two more reports for the MIQCP, *Ten Years of Public Building in Germany*, and, consolidating their frequent visits to Britain and knowledge of British architecture, *Ten Years of Public Building in Britain*. The following year they exhibited their work as part of a group show in Denmark and Sweden – their first overseas exhibitions. In 1990 they took their exhibition 'Maquettes Invraisemblables' to the VII Bienal de Arquitectura de Quito, Ecuador, as part of the section on 'New architectural tendencies in France and Europe: Deconstructivism', and the same year they received the Royal Society of Arts Ninth International Prize of Architecture for the BPO in London, and participated there in the Second Academy Architecture Forum on 'The New Modernism'. In France, their work was included in the Institut Français d'Architecture exhibition '40 Under 40', which over the next few years travelled to the Venice Biennale, Düsseldorf, Chicago and Tokyo. Since 1990 Decq and Cornette have consistently contributed to the architectural debate on the international circuit, and in 1995 they opened their first solo exhibition in the Aedes Gallery in Berlin.

Apart from exhibiting and discussing their own work, Decq and Cornette have also put a considerable effort into teaching, mainly in France (UP6/Paris La Villette, Grenoble, and the École Spéciale d'Architecture), but also at the University of Montreal, Canada, where Decq was visiting professor from 1991–92. Since 1985 they have welcomed into their office students, or 'stageurs', who come both from France and increasingly from abroad in search of the practical experience needed to fulfil the architecture course requirements, but also make a vital contribution to the maintenance of a lively spirit of enquiry from one project to the next.

Decq and Cornette's office today typifies the type of internationalism which is becoming increasingly common in the larger, more progressive architects' offices in Europe and America. Alongside the offices of Portzamparc, Nouvel, Wilmotte, Starck, Perrault and a few others, Decq and Cornette's has become one of the first ports of call for young foreign architects, often equipped only with the international language of architecture, seeking work in Paris at the forefront of the profession. Since completing the BPO, Decq and Cornette have regularly been invited not only to compete for major public projects throughout France against national and international rivals of the highest calibre, tending towards the more avant-garde, but also to sit on juries for other competitions. Although they recognize this as a function of the political system in France, and the need for competing regions to establish prestige through their building projects, it also provides a measure of French recognition of Decq and Cornette's established international profile.

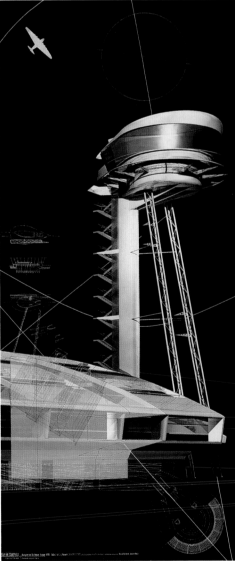

27

Although the French like to draw parallels between Decq and Cornette's architecture and British high tech, the similarities do not extend beyond construction technique and materials. Decq and Cornette criticize the lack of 'soul' in Foster's work, and it is precisely in the spirit of their work compared to that of the British high-tech architects that the glaring difference between them lies. From a conceptual point of view, there is a much closer relationship between Decq and Cornette's work and that of the British-based Iraqi architect Zaha Hadid. Hadid works in concrete rather than metal, and with planes rather than structure, but her architecture is inspired by the same ideas of kinetic energy and movement, and the working methods are very similar. Hadid too constructs her architecture along lines of force traced across a site, and the paintings she produces, which are so central to her architectural production, play an almost identical role to Decq and Cornette's models in expressing these ideas through a medium that falls somewhere between architecture and art.

The other British architect who produces work in a spirit close to that of Decq and Cornette's is Will Alsop, although his work tends towards the eccentric, while theirs tends towards the slick. If there is industrial imagery lurking in Alsop's work it is far more tempered by artistic form-making than in Decq and Cornette's. But in terms of materials and construction, he shares their predilection for metal, glass, and the precision that can be achieved working in that medium. Like them, his work is structurally and formally inventive, if not truly innovative, but Alsop's buildings are conceived essentially as static objects poised in space quite unlike the cinematic compositions of line and dynamic movement which Decq and Cornette produce.

As Decq and Cornette's work is not particularly characteristic of French contemporary architecture, neither is Hadid's nor Alsop's representative of mainstream architectural thought and practice in Britain. For all of them, the intellectual context in which they work is primarily a global one made up of an international community of architects committed to a serious questioning of the architectural status quo and pushing the discipline to its conceptual limits. Amongst them may also be counted kindred spirits such as Coop Himmelblau, Bernard Tschumi, Daniel Libeskind, Diller and Scofidio, Lebbeus Woods, Peter Eisenman, Peter Cook, Itsuko Hasegawa and others who constitute a loose international circuit interested in sustaining debate and comparing work.

While there is a pronounced academic bent to much of this inquiry, Decq and Cornette consciously maintain a fundamentally pragmatic stance, rooted in the principles of construction. Furthermore, while aspiring to participate actively in the international forum, and wishing to maintain a distance from the opposing camps of French architectural production, they are ultimately based firmly within the French system which has nurtured them, despite their unconcealed opposition to a deeply ingrained Beaux-Arts sensibility. It seems most likely that their future role in the story of contemporary architecture will depend to a great extent on how far they can maintain a platform of influence within the French system without sacrificing the deliberate ambiguity of their position, in the face of considerable pressure to fit in; and how effectively they manage to use that platform as a basis for valuable ambassadorial work between the French and international architectural forums.

Notes
1 *Architecture Intérieure Crée*, 8–9, 1990, p 130: MHC.
2 The new schools of the Université de Paris were numbered 1–8, UP1 being the former architectural department of the École des Beaux-Arts.
3 See Boudon's papers *Architecture Architecturologie. II. Systèmes*, DGRST 1975; *Architecture Architecturologie. III. Analyses*, DRGST 1975; *Figuration Graphique en Architecture: Architecture des sigles*, DGRST 1976; *Figuration Graphique en Architecture: Le théâtre de la figuration*, DRGST 1976; and *Intégration et Architecture*, Area, Corda, 1976.
4 See *Les Mécanismes de la commande Publique d'Architecture en R F A*, report, 1978.
5 *Identité Urbaine: La Reconstruction de 5 Villes Allemandes après la Guerre 1939–1945*, report, 1979.
6 *Albums de la Jeune Architecture, Odile Decq (Benoît Cornette)*, Ministre de l'Equipement, du Logement, de l'Aménagement du Territoire et des Transports, 1986.
7 'Hyper-Tension': text to accompany the exhibit at the Centre National d'Art Contemporain, Grenoble, 1993.
8 *Ibid.*
9 *Maquettes Invraisemblables: 'The Model is the Message'*, exhibition catalogue (Showroom Artemide, Paris, 27 November–17 December 1989).
10 *Ibid.*
11 As quoted by Bernard Tschumi in his Academy Lecture, 13 June 1992, in *Theory and Experimentation*, ed by A Papadakis (London: Academy Editions, 1993).
12 Text written for presentation at the Academy Forum discussion, 'Theory and Experimentation', 13 June 1992.
13 *Ibid.*
14 *Ibid.*

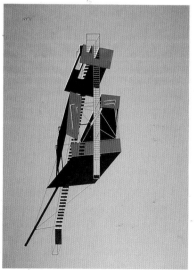

28 Un Signal at La Défense, 1991, model showing interrelationship of elements.

28

PROJECTS

1 Aerial view of the model, with linear axes exaggerated to emphasize the geometry and the in-between space of the scheme.
2, 3 Ground floor plan and exploded axonometric view showing cut-back facade with the cash lobby immediately behind and the interconnecting spaces of the office and tiny covered courtyard.
4 View of the model, showing the key elements: the facade, cash dispensers, the roof over the courtyard and the wall between the cash lobby and office.

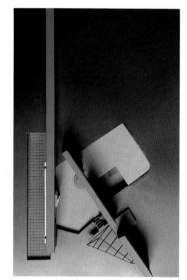

1

Crédit Agricole
Mayenne
1982–83

This is a small but surprising intervention in the historic centre of Mayenne, capital of the rural French province of the same name. The $75m^2$ space for an automatic banking facility was originally a shop, and the brief was to turn it into a cash point lobby with a small room behind for 'telephone appointments' between the bank's customers and staff, which would be open once a week. Although the cash point has been very successful, the telephone service has now been closed, in response to the reaction against total automation of functions.

The treatment of the shopfront demonstrates the layering of surface, designed to emphasize the process of movement from an external to an internal space, which was to become typical of Decq and Cornette's work. The window, slightly recessed within a heavy stone-clad frame suggesting a rusticated portico, curves back gently to increase the sense of depth in the street frontage, and to form a contrast with the stiff rigour of the frame. The glass is divided into sections by a grid of thick glazing bars, giving the impression of a portcullis, and playing on the dichotomy between the desire to give an appearance of transparency and easy entrance, and the need for security, both real and perceived. The entrance itself is marked by a single *pilotis* partially enclosed in a fluted, broken column – the most pointed statement in the ironic or humorous commentary on architectural language which simmers beneath the surface of the project.

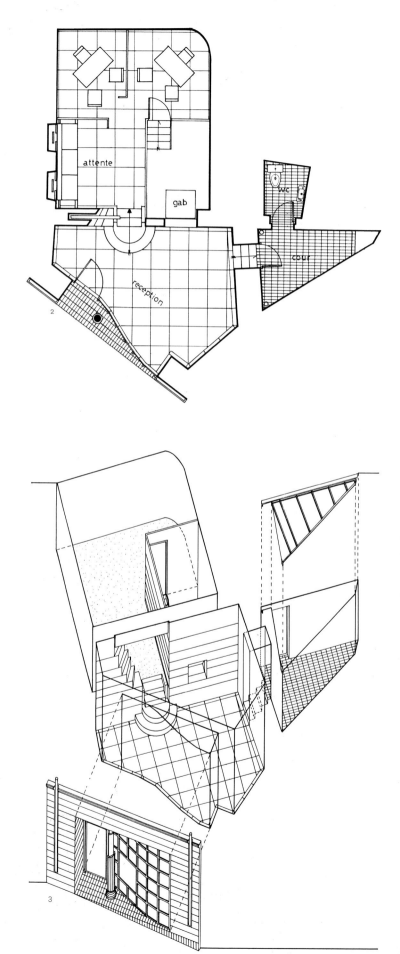

2

3

4

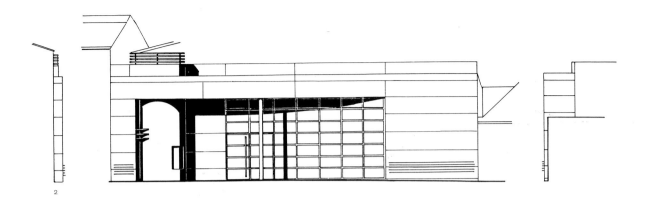

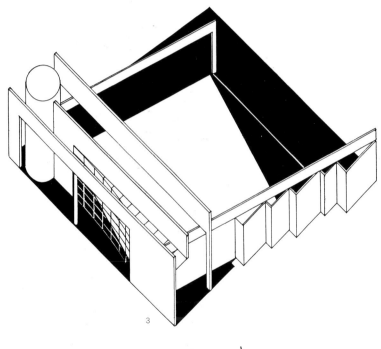

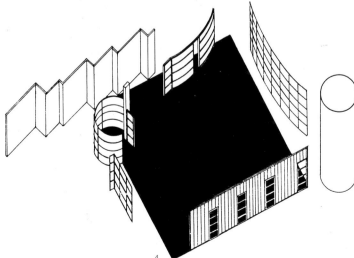

Crédit Mutuel

Laval

1986–87

This was a scheme for a bank interior in Laval. It provides an open-plan layout, as requested by the client, articulated by a small circular enclosure towards the back of the space, designed for private meetings, and another circular structural element embedded in the front facade, containing services. A series of partitioned cellular units open to the main space is set against the outer side wall.

The overall geometry is slightly skewed, reflecting the awkward shape of the site. The front facade is treated in a very similar manner to the Crédit Agricole scheme, as a multi-layered series of screens forming a clear spatial progression between the external world and the interior space. The outermost facade forms a frame to the whole composition, while the entrance itself opens through a gently curving screen slightly set back behind the frame, creating a sliver of additional public space at the edge of the street. The development of this aspect of the scheme reflects the discussions taking place at that time about the facade as volume, rather than merely skin or envelope.

1 Aerial view of the model, with its geometry mapped out by yellow lines; cellular spaces along one side and two circular elements articulate the orthogonal layout. The front elevation below shows the facade's layering and the circular service drum protruding through the frame.
2, 3, 4 Elevation (fig 2), and bird's-eye axonometric (figs 3, 4) demonstrate the concept of the dissociation of elements as central to the design process.

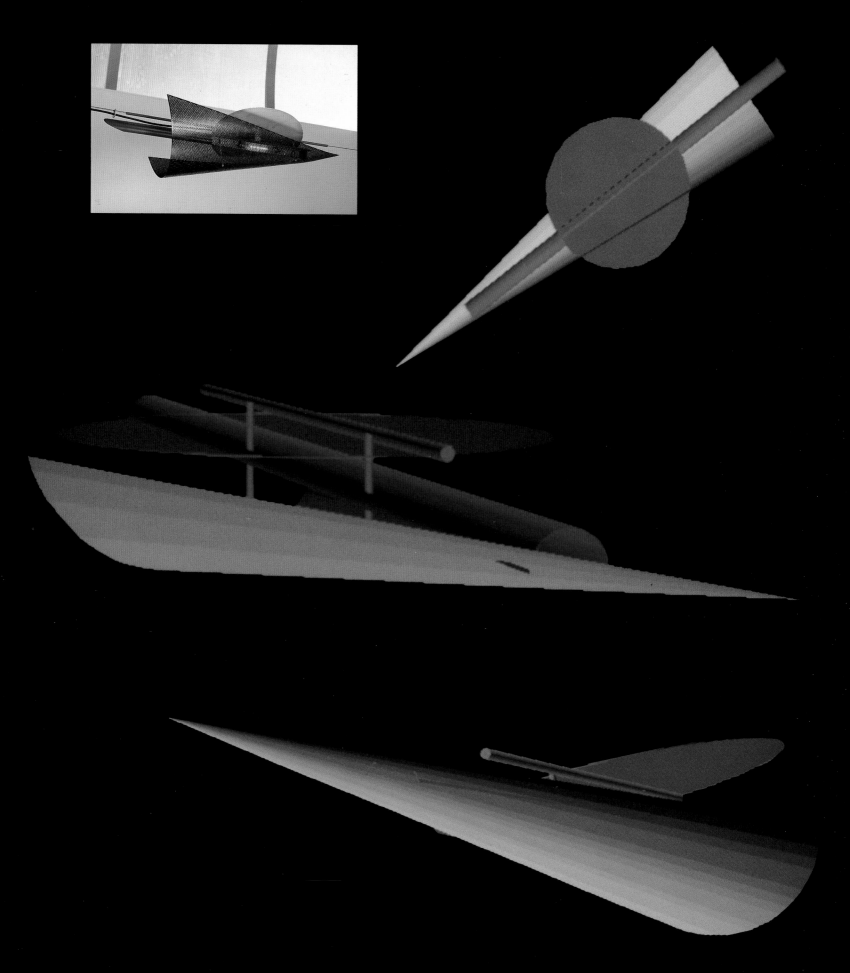

2   3   4

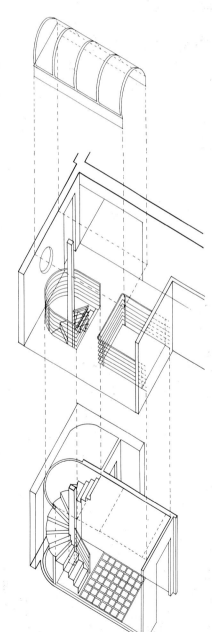

Cinéma et Communication

Paris

1987–88

This headquarters for a production company is located on the fifth and sixth floor of a Haussmannian building in Paris, right under the roof. The link between the two floors is created by a twisted metal and timber stair, underneath a large skylight. The flow of natural light through the roof helps to expand the sense of space in what would otherwise be cramped attic accommodation, and encourages the use of the central 'courtyard' area as an informal gathering point.

The sense of light and space is enhanced by the choice of transparent or semi-transparent partition walls between the offices located on each floor. Natural light is complemented by artificial light from various sources, notably a special lamp fitting inspired by the American surveillance aircraft, 'AWACS', which is suspended underneath the skylight and moves around the central space on runners – the crowning stylistic flourish of the scheme.

1 Details of the light fitting suspended beneath the central skylight. The light is an abstracted representation of the American surveillance plane 'AWACS'.

2, 3, 4 Interior views showing the curving stairwell with its refined metal balustrade, emerging underneath the skylight into a bright central gathering point on the upper floor.

5 Bird's-eye axonometric showing the interrelationship between the floors and barrelvault skylight.

5

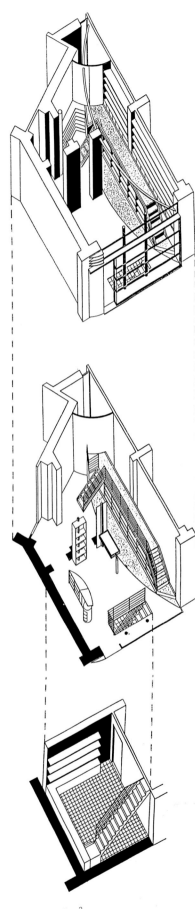

1 Model of the interior highlighting the play between the curved line of tension demarcating the self-service area, and the angular geometry of the site.

2 Bird's-eye axonometric showing the connecting stair to the basement (bottom), and the ground floor sales zone (middle and top). The open plan is articulated by freestanding fittings (shown middle) and the clearly legible structure (shown top).

3, 4 The curved geometry connects the public front of the shop and sales area with the private office at the back.

5, 6 Sketches, as with Decq and Cornette's models, are coloured to indicate the materials and structure.

3

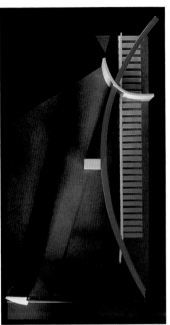

4

Stationer's

Avenue Franklin D Roosevelt, Paris
1987

This proposal again explores the relationship between curved and rectilinear geometries. The project was for a client moving into new premises and wishing to modernize the layout and image of the former shop: an old-fashioned stationer's in which there was limited free circulation and goods had to be requested across the counter and retrieved by assistants.

The new shop is an open-plan space, incorporating a main sales area with freestanding display units, and a self-service storage system forming a raised gallery along one side. The two areas are demarcated by a curved line of tension inscribed by a lighting rail suspended below the ceiling, and contrasting floor surfaces. The curved geometry extends back throughout the space from the window to the innermost corner, in which is located a small office, transforming the funnel-like narrowing of the volume from a disadvantage into a deliberate formal feature.

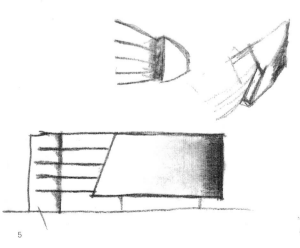

2

5

6

1, 2, 3 The facade of
Decq and Cornette's
housing on rue Manin
represents a dialectic
between surface,
emphasized by the tile
cladding, and depth,
generated by cutting
into the skin to reveal
its thickness. The

axonometric shows
how the facade fits
against the structure of
the building.
4 Model exhibited as
part of 'Maquettes
Invraisemblables'
showing the layering
of the wall planes.
The perspectival view

along the facade, as
seen from the street,
has an anamorphic
appearance.

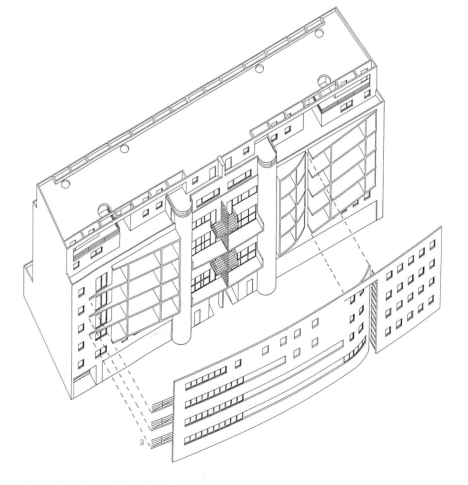

2

1

Social Housing
Rue Manin, Paris
1987–89

Critic Martin Mead singled out the model
of this scheme for comment in
his contribution to the catalogue
accompanying Decq and Cornette's
exhibition 'Maquettes Invraisemblables:
the Model is the Message'. The model
described a layering of wall planes, in
exaggerated perspective, which focuses
attention on the active role of the facade
and entrance in defining the relationship

between internal and external space.
Part of the reason for focusing so closely
on the nature of the facade in this project
was the imposition of tight restrictions
on plan, volume and materials by the
masterplan for the overall development
on this 'ZAC' controlled area ('zone
d'amenagement concerté') close to the
Parc de la Villette. This left only the
facade free as a zone for exploration and
architectural expression.

Decq and Cornette's interest in the
nature of entry into a building dates back
to their early interior projects, and the

desire to express the process of
transition from one world into another
through more than just the opening and
closing of a door. In this scheme they
explore the facade of the building in
terms of a layering of vertical plans,
rather than a simple screen. The curved
outermost layer is superimposed against
the rectilinear plan of the inner layer, the
asymmetry of the former contrasting with
the symmetrical positioning of the central
public entry and the projecting stairwells
placed either side in the latter.

3

4

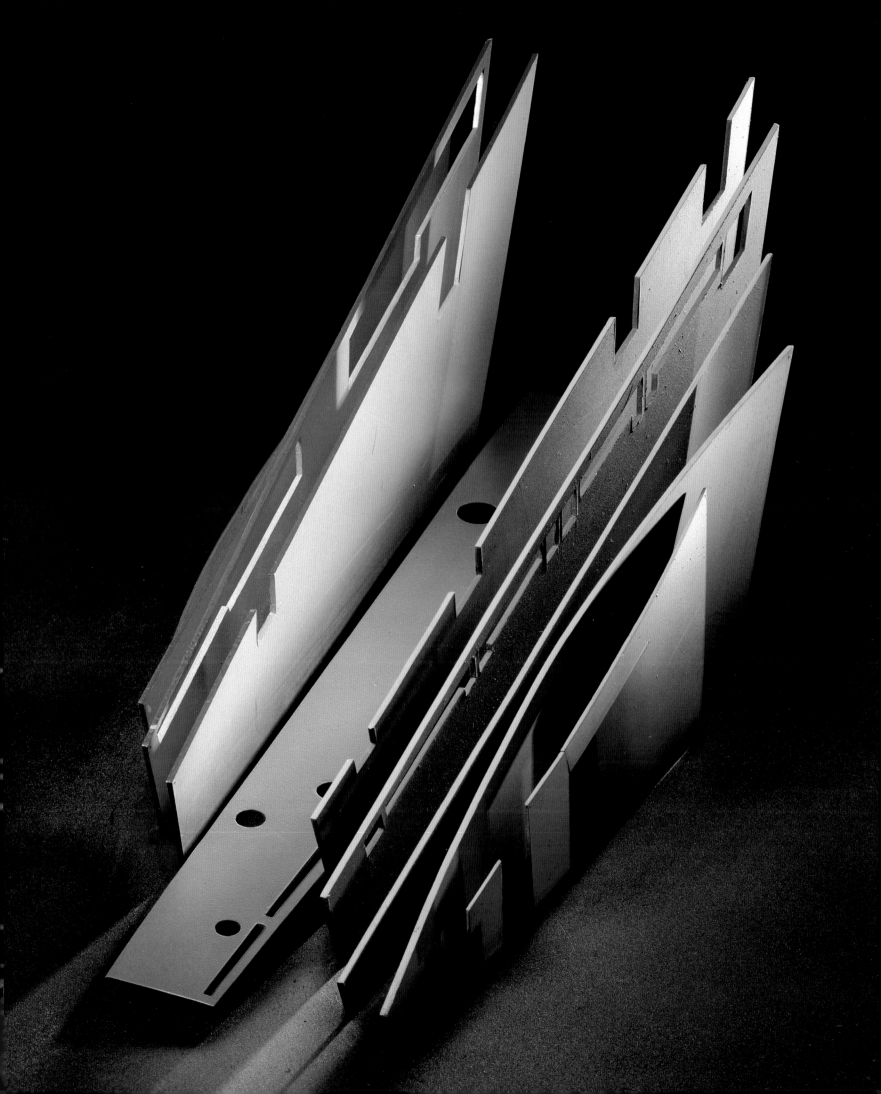

5

6

5 Detail showing the perforation of the roof edge, allowing for an increased play of light at the top of the building, and revealing the duplex flats at the top as private 'villas' on the roof.

6 Detail showing the juncture of the facade's outermost layer with that immediately behind.

7 View of the front facade, animated by shadows and the silhouettes of trees.

DECQ CORNETTE

8

DECQ CORNETTE

8 View from the rooftop
looking down onto the
skylights behind the
screen-like facade.

9 Floorplans showing
the symmetrical layout of
the apartments.

10 View showing the
private external areas
treated as double-height
loggias behind the outer
skin of the facade.

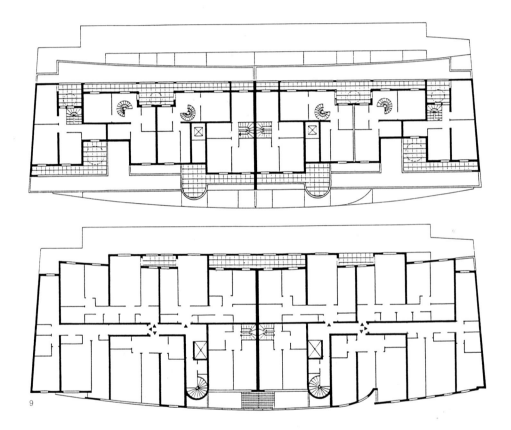

9

10

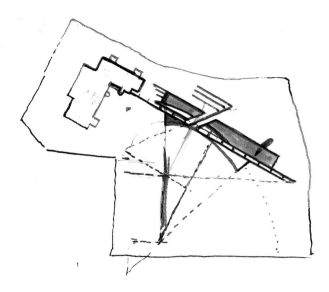

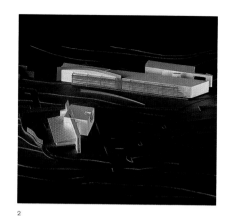

1 Sketch diagram of the site and force lines across it, with the existing building at left, and the proposed new structure at right.
2 Sketch models of the scheme located on the site.
3 Distorted axonometric: drawing becomes a medium through which to explore the dissociation of elements and the energy this can bring into the scheme.
4 Model diagram of the site with the proposed structures located according to the force lines mapped across it.

Banque Populaire de l'Ouest

Administrative and Social Centres

Montgermont, Rennes

1988–90

The Administrative Centre building of the Banque Populaire de l'Ouest – or BPO – complex at Montgermont, outside Rennes, has an immediate visual impact from the highway along the edge of the site. Its double-glazed suspended glass facade, supported laterally by an external metal structure two metres in front, creates a shimmering screen running parallel with the road. Engineered by the British engineering company Rice Francis Ritchie it was the first example of its kind to be constructed in France.

It drew enormous press attention at the time of the building's completion and won a number of awards.

Decq and Cornette resist the critics' labelling of the building as high tech in the British style, although they admit that they had to travel to Britain to view similar structures, such as Nicholas Grimshaw's Financial Times Printing Works or Richard Rogers' Lloyds and Reuters buildings, in the face of claims by a certain French magazine that their concept could never be realized. They have also consciously rejected the application to their work of the term 'high tech', and substituted it by 'soft technology', to express an idea of an advanced and sophisticated form of

structural technology implemented not for the sake of technology itself, but as the means of achieving a very particular quality of transparency and light: the architectural poetics of the building.

The decision to use glass and metal for the building was taken in the first place for reasons of precision, and also as a response to the client's anxiety about the structural integrity of the glass and preference for concrete. It was not deliberately intended as an exercise in 'breaking the system', but as the most effective way of achieving the desired architectural result. The entire structure was prefabricated off-site and assembled in a rapid eleven-month construction process, despite being

beset by problems. These were largely due to the inexperience of the small and medium-sized local firms (clients of the bank) working on the project, although lack of time – one year for preliminary studies and design, and two months for the production of all working drawings – was also an important factor. Nevertheless, the result is a building of high quality that makes a clear statement about the image of the bank as a forward-looking organization, and that also provides a pleasant, comfortable environment to work in and to visit.

The question of image was inherent to the brief from the earliest stages. Faced by increasing competition at the end of the 1980s, the BPO formulated a new

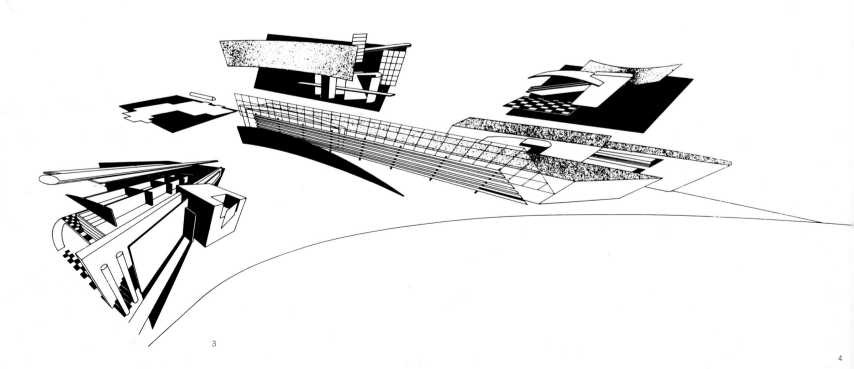

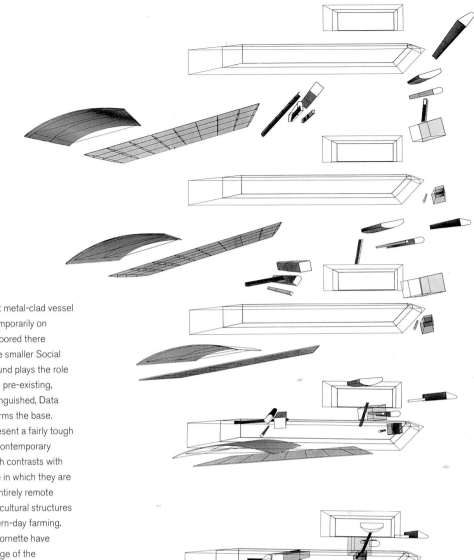

development initiative for the 1990s
based on the principles of optimum
performance, technological innovation,
and the cultivation of a business culture.
It went under the slogan of 'a bank which
forges ahead'. The new buildings were
intended very much to be a statement of
that identity, embodying efficient service,
professionalism, innovation, warmth of
reception, and the values of a corporate
enterprise operating at an essentially
human scale. They would also be highly
visible from the main road in and out of
Rennes. When the competition for a
design was launched it was clear that
the jury would be looking for something
reasonably image-conscious.

Decq and Cornette's design for the
Administrative Centre clearly draws on

the imagery of a great metal-clad vessel
which has alighted temporarily on
the site rather than moored there
permanently, while the smaller Social
Centre in the foreground plays the role
of gatehouse, and the pre-existing,
architecturally undistinguished, Data
Processing Centre forms the base.
The new buildings present a fairly tough
but streamlined and contemporary
industrial image, which contrasts with
the bucolic landscape in which they are
set, while not being entirely remote
from the types of agricultural structures
associated with modern-day farming.
However Decq and Cornette have
stressed that 'the image of the
building is not sacred'.

The dramatic transparent glass facade

6

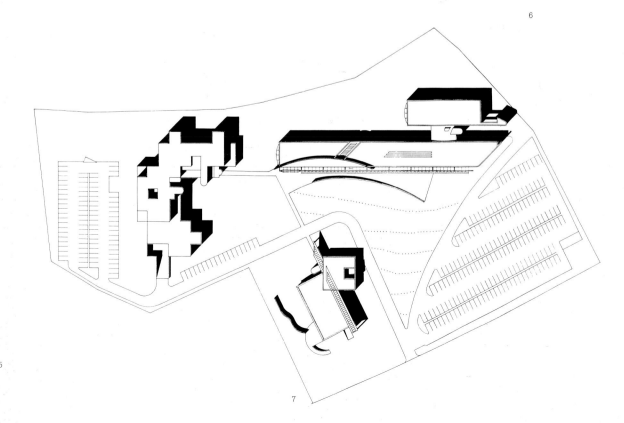

5

8

9

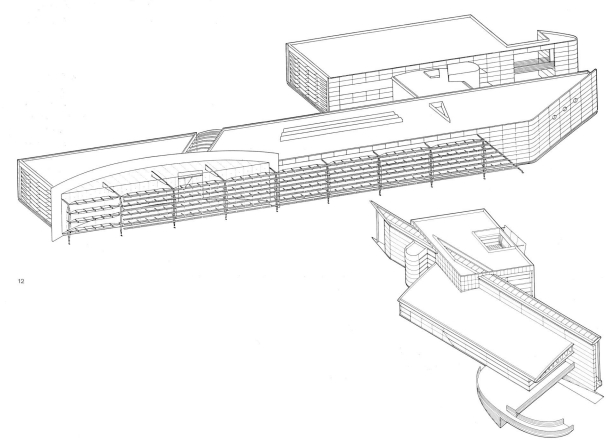

10

11

8 View of the front elevation from the west.

9 View of the front elevation from the east.

10 First floor plan.

11 Ground floor plan.

12 Axonometric view of the scheme showing the relationship between the two buildings.

12

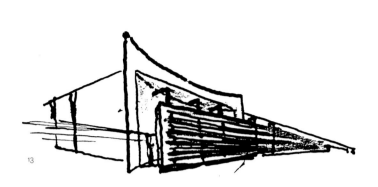

is not intended in the first place as a visual statement, but rather to enable the users of the building to see out onto the rural landscape, and to remove any element of mystery or secretiveness surrounding the internal workings of the bank. Above all it was the concept of the building as process, over and above image, which was the driving force behind the design approach.

This is summed up in the idea of the factory, or production line, which provided the inspiration for a plan intended to delineate a sequence of operations rather than present a static architectural set-piece. This entailed a destructuring of the programme, realized architecturally by the dissociation and then reconnection of the various functional elements. The key to the scheme lay in the mode of arrival – almost exclusively by car – on the site. The car park is set prominently to the front of the site, giving strong representation to the presence of the human work force. It is laid out in such a way as to extend the lines of the geometry traced by the two buildings. The route from the car park to the offices becomes the hinge between the two buildings on the east–west axis. In the early stages of the design process, the entrance to the Administrative Centre was pulled out and away from the building to disengage it from the rest of the building mass, but later, partly for reasons of cost, pushed back to form an integral, but distinct part inside the building.

Although the actual surface area of this prestigious hall is very small, the visual and physical effect is one of loftiness and length, created by the attenuated plan, and the curved back wall of shimmering lacquered aluminium brick, which passes through the external wall of the building at the far end and projects beyond it to form a sheltering screen for the entrance. The curve generates a dynamic counterpoint to the straight front elevation. The two-metre gap between the transparent, veil-like glass wall and the metal supporting structure is modelled on the traditional Italian arcade (as, for example, in Piazza San Marco, Venice), creating a channel of cooling air along the whole front of the building, and also a greater depth to the facade so that it becomes a space in itself, not simply a two-dimensional screen. This separation of the visual and physical limits of the building allows the entrance to be expressed as a passage in time between outside and inside space in which the threshold becomes a transitional space between the two rather than a simple boundary. The *brise-soleils* in the external supporting structure create changing patterns of light and shadow across the 9m-high, double-height hall which itself creates another layer of ambivalent

13, 14 Sketches of the Administrative Centre: perspective view from the west and aerial view.
15 Site plan showing the geometry of the site organization.

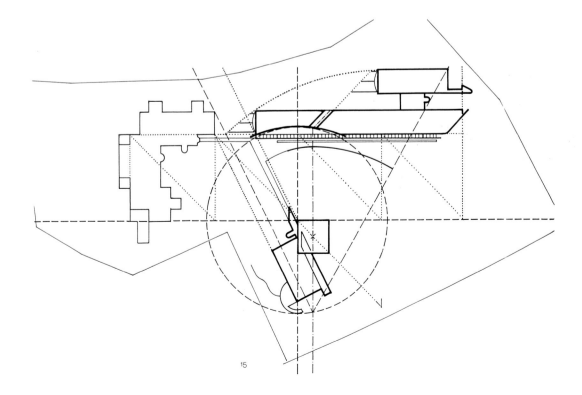

16   Detail of the front facade of the Administrative Centre from the west, viewed by night.

16

17 Administrative
Centre: interior view of
the main hall from the
entrance, showing the
blurring of visual and
physical boundaries.
18, 19 Perspective
views through the main
hall showing the
construction principles.
20 (overleaf)
Administrative Centre:
view of the entrance
to the rear of the
main block, with the
curved stair-tower
at right.

18

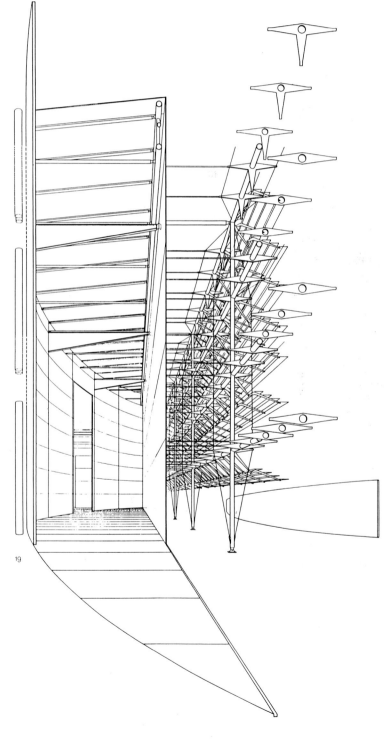

19

17

20 (overleaf)

21

22

23

24

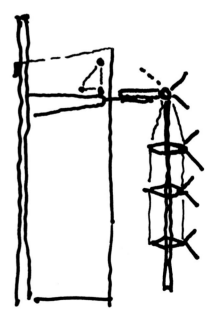

25

21 Interior views showing the bridge link between the front and rear blocks.
22, 23 Interior views showing the glazed lift in the link section (fig 22) and the quality of the office spaces (fig 23).
24 View from the main hall into the reception area showing the stair to the upper level and views through the building's glazed rear facade.
25 Sketch diagram illustrating the connection between the detached glass and metal facade and the main building structure.
26 Diagram showing the construction of the floor slabs and location of services in the Administrative Centre.
27, 28 Sections through the Administrative Centre taken through the main entrance hall (fig 27) and through the offices (fig 28).

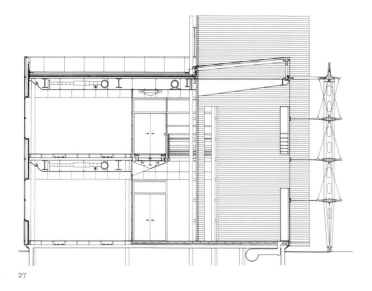

27

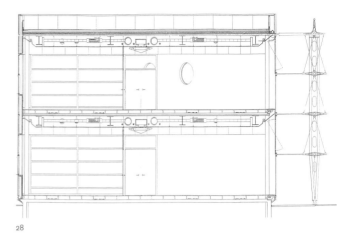

28

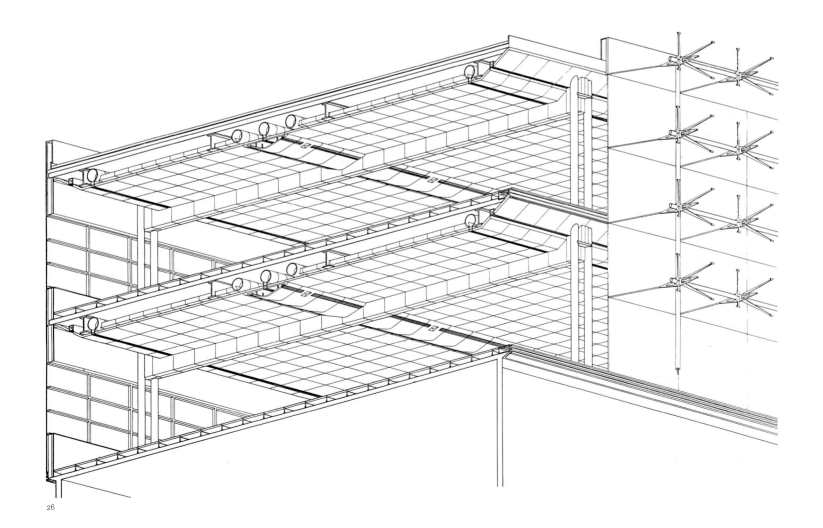

26

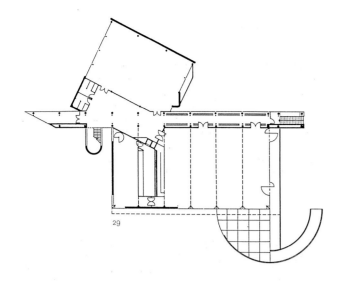

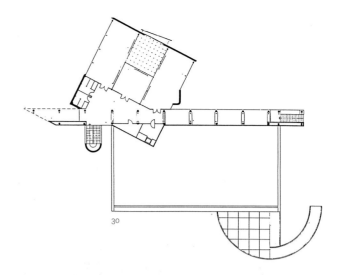

29

30

indoor/outdoor territory to be traversed before the building proper is entered through the curved screen at the other end from the main entrance door.

The treatment of the hall as a promenade, creating an immediate sense of movement through the building, is very important to the whole idea of 'parcours' as the generating force for the organization of the spaces. The brief had asked that these be planned for maximum flexibility of use, and also with the highest possible level of transparency, for ease of communication between the different parts of the organization. In fact the footprint of the building is very simple: two orthogonal forms alongside each other (the one

behind is much smaller and was added into the brief after the competition), connected by a transparent glass hall in which the communal functions of the building (coffee machines, photocopiers, smoking area etc) are concentrated. Each volume is constructed on a grid generated by a 12m x 13.20m module, into which are inserted service nodes forming points of articulation between the open-plan office spaces and the circulation areas and gathering points.

The ground floor of the main building is occupied by the reception area and ancillary offices at one end, and at the other the machinery for cheque-processing running along the front half of the building – literally a production

line. On the upper floor, reached by a freestanding staircase in the reception area, open-plan office space filling the whole length and width of the building is entered off a gallery looking down into the reception area. The west facade is glazed, framing a view of the Data Processing Centre; the east end of the building forms a point, suggesting a culmination of the flow of movement set in motion by the entrance hall. The slightly nautical overtones of the shape are emphasized by three round port-holes punched into the metal-clad exterior wall.

The smaller building contains a single space on each floor. At the upper level it is connected to the main building across

the glazed hall by a bridge linked to a staircase down to ground level. The staircase is contained in a projecting curved staircase tower adjacent to the entrance. On the other side, the glazed wall of the hall frames a vista towards the Data Processing Base along the sheer rear facade of the front building, the base marked with a black band to reinforce an impression of lightness and detachment from the ground.

The entrance to the Social Centre is set on the diagonal north–south axis with the Administrative Centre, and the axis is continued through the building to form an internal gallery with a glazed wall giving views out onto the car park and surrounding landscape. This route can be

31

29, 30 Ground and first floor plans of the Social Centre. The geometry is generated by the collision of two rectilinear boxes.
31 Social Centre, view from the northwest, with the entrance canopy projecting prominently to welcome visitors and frame views of the landscape beyond.
32 Social Centre, view from the road. The roof over the restaurant building is shaped like an aeroplane wing, while the circulation spine between the two main volumes projects out towards the landscape marking the presence of the building on the road.

32

33

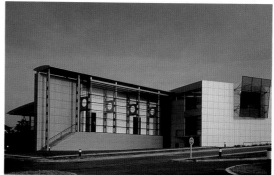

34

33, 34 Social Centre, view from the Administrative Centre (fig 33), and detailed view of gallery promenade showing the restaurant, and the metal screen shielding the directors' roof terrace at first floor level (fig 34).

35, 36 Elevational treatments of the Social Centre (clockwise): from the carpark, the Administrative Centre, the road, and the west. 37 Close-up view of the metal screen in front of the roof terrace.

clearly read as a narrow linear volume passing between the two juxtaposed rectangular volumes set at a slight angle to each other which make up the bulk of the building. The accommodation consists of a spacious staff restaurant on the ground floor, looking out towards the road and the countryside beyond, which occupies the whole of one single-storey block. The second volume, on the other side of the central axis, contains the entrance hall and training rooms on the ground floor. On the first floor, reached by a staircase which is again expressed as a projecting curved stair-tower on the exterior of the building, are dining facilities for directors and their visitors served by a small

kitchen. A small roof terrace behind a metal screen looks out over the car park, allowing the directors of the bank to survey the ranks of their personnel from an elevated position.

Neither building is air-conditioned, in accordance with the wishes of the client. A system of air circulation, extraction and replacement was installed instead, and careful attention paid to thermal control of the glazed front facade by means of the *brise-soleils* placed externally, allowing air to circulate between the supporting structure and the glass wall itself. Despite the metal structure, sound insulation is of a high quality, achieved by the installation of an extremely dense carpeting material, and micro-perforation

of ceiling tiles and wall coverings.

The construction of the BPO would not have been possible on any site nearer the centre of town, both from the point of view of space and from the point of view of planning controls. The planning zone around Montgermont is free of controls, and, furthermore, the scheme was supported by the government department for historic monuments on the grounds that bank buildings throughout the world were setting important precedents for avant-garde architecture, and therefore represented a suitable building type for architectural experimentation. As the first metal office building to be constructed in France, apart from the Institut du Monde Arabe

by Jean Nouvel in Paris, the BPO became, in its way, a *cause célèbre* among those interested in shaking off the trammels of the Beaux-Arts tradition and all that it was identified with.

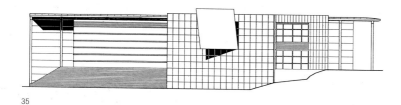

35

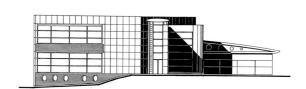

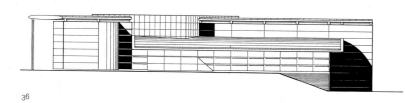

36

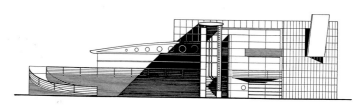

37

1

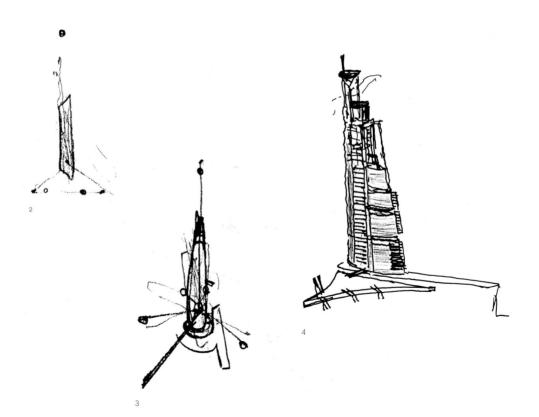

2

3

4

DECQ CORNETTE

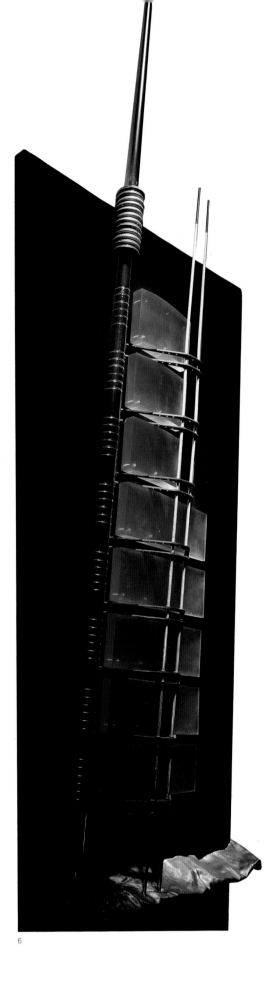

1 Perspective view of Triangle de la Folie in context, showing its relationship to the Grande Arche (centre) and CNIT building (right). The verticality of the tower contrasts with the squat volume of the CNIT building.

2, 3, 4 Sketches show explorations of orientation and geometry.
5 Early concept sketch.
6 View of the model, showing how the supporting structure is placed on the exterior of the building.

Triangle de la Folie

La Défense, Paris

1988

Decq and Cornette's submission for the competition finally won by Jean Nouvel's Tour sans Fin was inspired by various non-architectural images. The overall composition is modelled on the form of a 100m-long upended aeroplane wing, or metal blade, supported by an external mast based on a ship's mast. It is also compared to a lighthouse, pointing its antennae towards space and the satellites.

The decision to place the supporting structure on the outside of the building was reached as the most appropriate and economic solution to a technical problem of stability caused by the height of the tower.

The body of the building – or fuselage – consists of office accommodation grouped in seven-storey cantilevered blocks, each slightly shorter in length than the preceding block. The gradual shortening of the projection from the mast, which contains the high-speed lifts, allowed its height to be increased. This was important because the tower was conceived as a landmark at the entry to Paris, on a triangular site between the railway line and Neuilly cemetery, which would form part of a triptych at the so-called Tête Défense consisting of the tower, the Grande Arche, and the CNIT building (Centre National des Industries et des Techniques/Cité des Affaires). The intermediate floors between each block contain the communal spaces. At the top of the building are VIP areas and a roof terrace, and crowning the structure is technical plant and a communications network facilitating contact with the rest of the world.

While the design is formally and structurally expressive, it was conceived as a considered and pragmatic response to the needs specified in the programme. High levels of natural light are achieved by limiting the depth of the office floors, and the manner in which the floors are divided is intended to allow maximum flexibility of occupation.

6

5

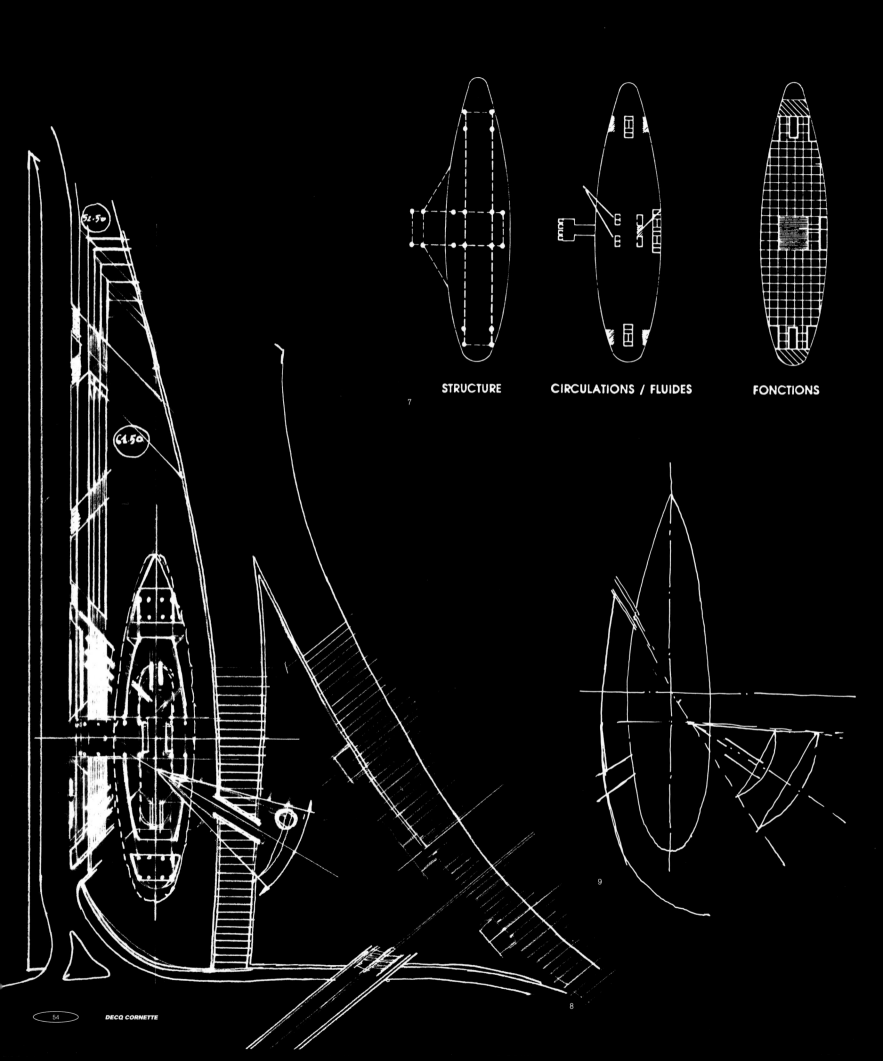

STRUCTURE   CIRCULATIONS / FLUIDES   FONCTIONS

7

9

8

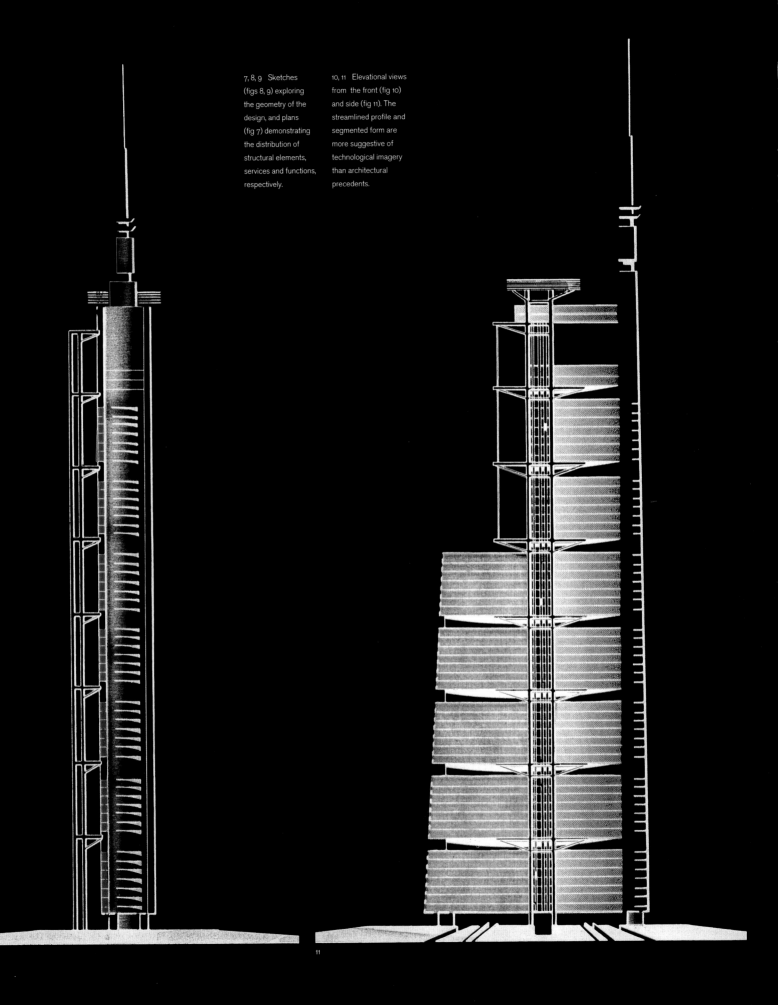

7, 8, 9 Sketches
(figs 8, 9) exploring
the geometry of the
design, and plans
(fig 7) demonstrating
the distribution of
structural elements,
services and functions,
respectively.

10, 11 Elevational views
from the front (fig 10)
and side (fig 11). The
streamlined profile and
segmented form are
more suggestive of
technological imagery
than architectural
precedents.

10

11

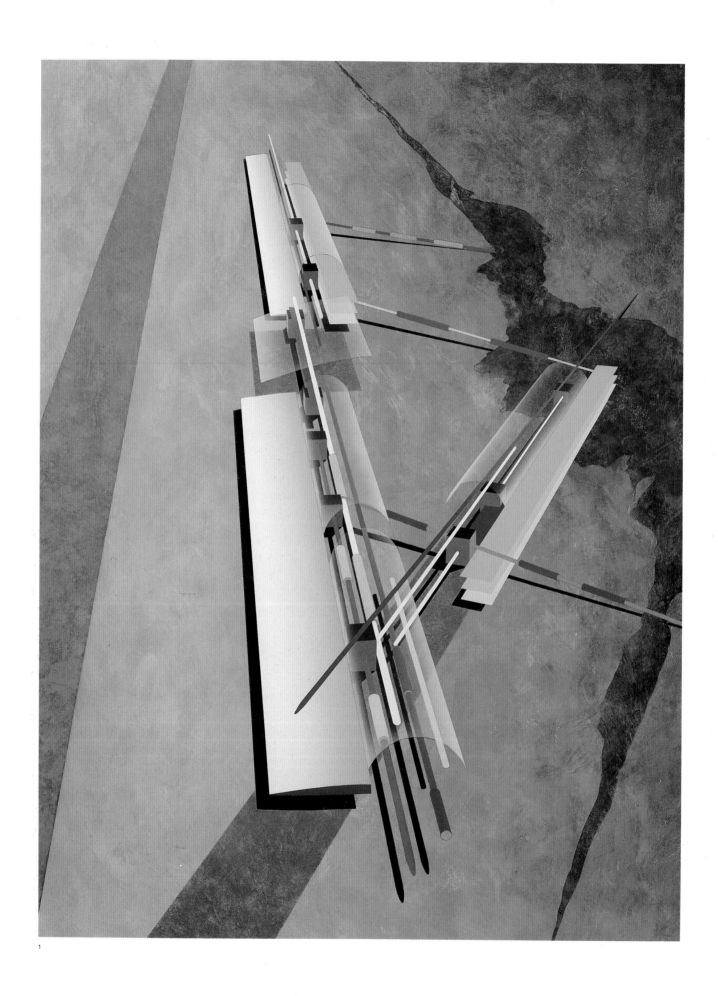

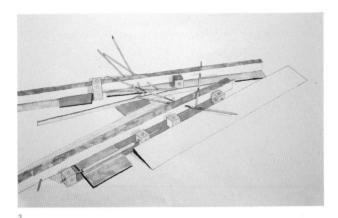

2

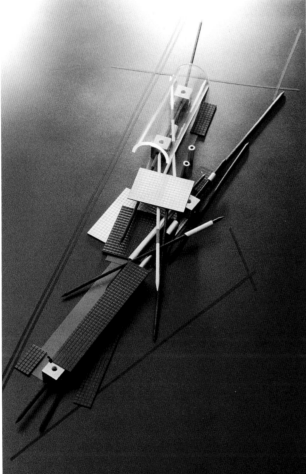

3

4

Apple Computer France Headquarters
St Quentin-en-Yvelines
1989

'The Apple ship is an orbital station …
set to take off into the future. It is the
mother vessel at the heart of the ACF
(Apple Computer France) galaxy, which
allows those who enter it to plunge into
the infinite space of communication.'

The site for this project was a business
park in the new town of St Quentin-en-
Yvelines near Paris. In response to
the size of the site and the absence
of existing context or any planning
framework, Decq and Cornette used a
game of chance – pik-stiks, or spilikins –
to formulate the shape and orientation of
the building. They allowed the spilikins to
fall at random across a model of the site,
and used the resulting configuration as a
basic framework for the construction of
axes which would determine the form of
the building: a process of creating order
out of apparent chaos. The exercise was
intended to demonstrate the limitations
of a fixed methodology of site occupation
dependent on the existence of context,
and the necessity of entertaining a
flexible approach capable of responding
to each particular set of circumstances
on its own terms.

The imagery cited as inspiration for
the project demonstrates Decq and
Cornette's interest in using material
derived from other areas of cultural and
technological development to generate
architectural ideas. The scheme itself
is based on the concept of a series of
nodes which play the role of synapses in
the nervous system. These comprise the
crossing-points of the vertical and
horizontal elements of the circulation
and structural system, the services, the
communal spaces, and the points of
convergence between the different
worlds which make up the Apple
organization. They are connected by
walkways, ramps and other forms of
circulation space, the principle of the
scheme being the construction of a
flexible armature, capable of extension
or contraction, by which the different
functions of the building are connected.

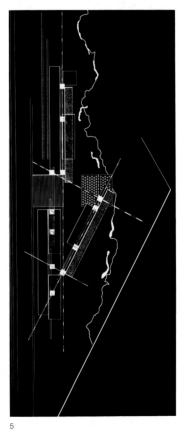

5

6 *(overleaf)*

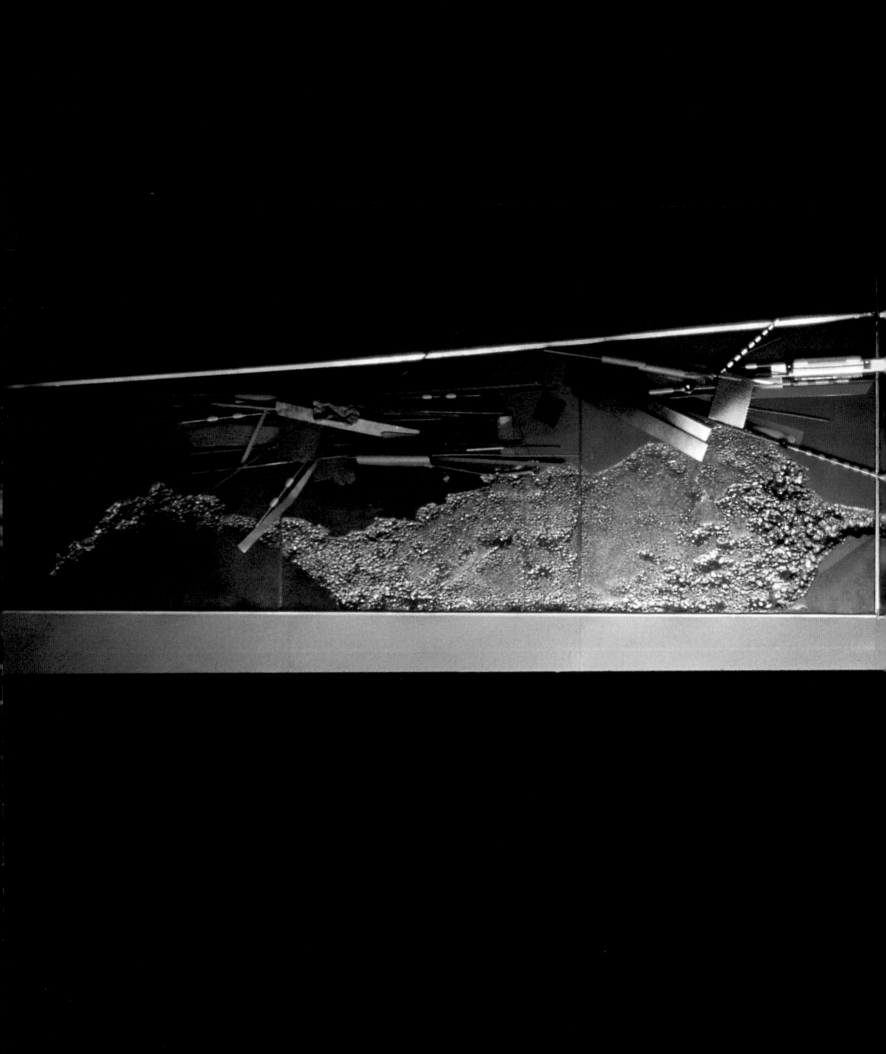

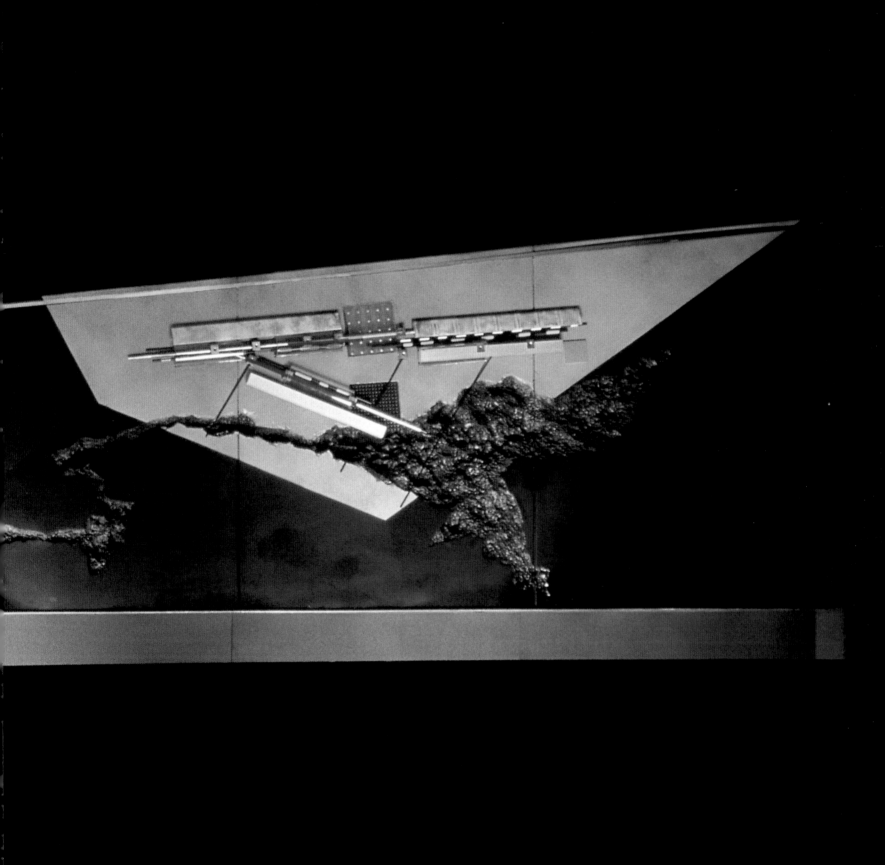

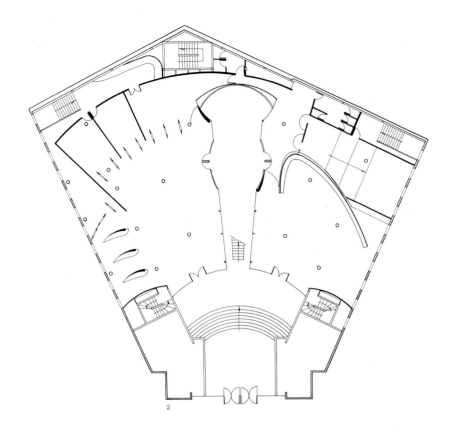

2

1 Office interior; fin-like aluminium partitions can be moved to provide alternative ways of dividing the showroom space.
2 Ground floor plan showing open-plan spaces surrounded by fringes of more meeting room and ancillary provisions.
3, 4 Interior views reveal the continuous flow of space in both visual and physical terms.

Apple Computer France Showroom

Nantes

1989–90

This scheme for Apple consisted of the conversion of an old biscuit factory into new offices, conference facilities and showrooms. The plan is divided into two parts either side of a central circulation channel, which acts as a filter into the surrounding space. On each side are open exhibition areas fringed by service spaces: a demonstration room, training facilities, meeting rooms, a dining room, conference room, lavatories and vertical circulation, tucked into the perimeter of the building. The shiny metallic surfaces and fin-like partitions evoke a sub sci-fi aesthetic not inappropriate to a centre for computer technology.

3

4

5

6

5, 6 Interior views. The
workstations are tucked
behind the metal fins.
7, 8 Drawings explore
the construction of
curving, freestanding
perimeter screens.

9 Construction details
of fin partitions showing
the attachment of the
workstation fixture.

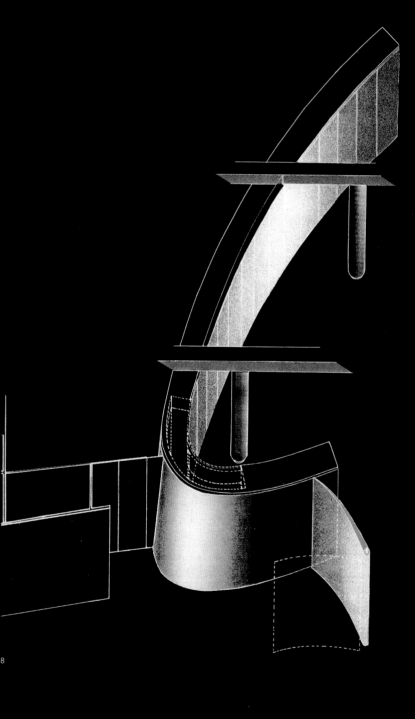

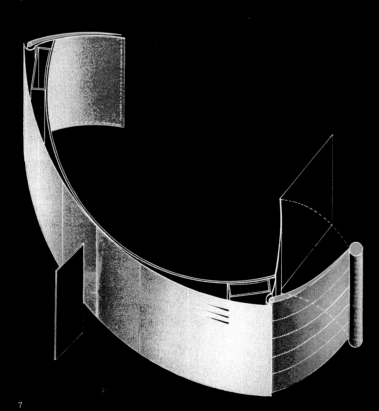

7

8

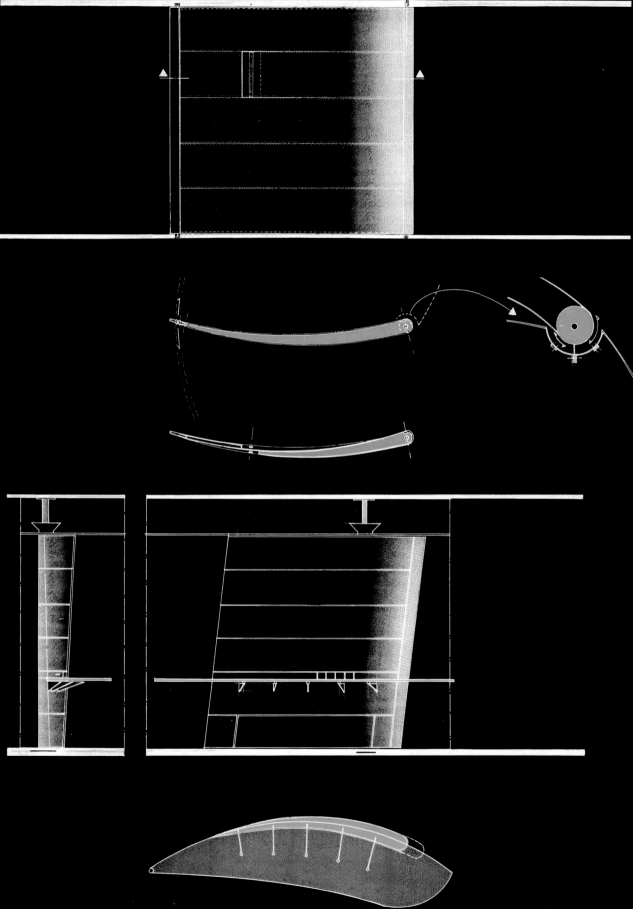

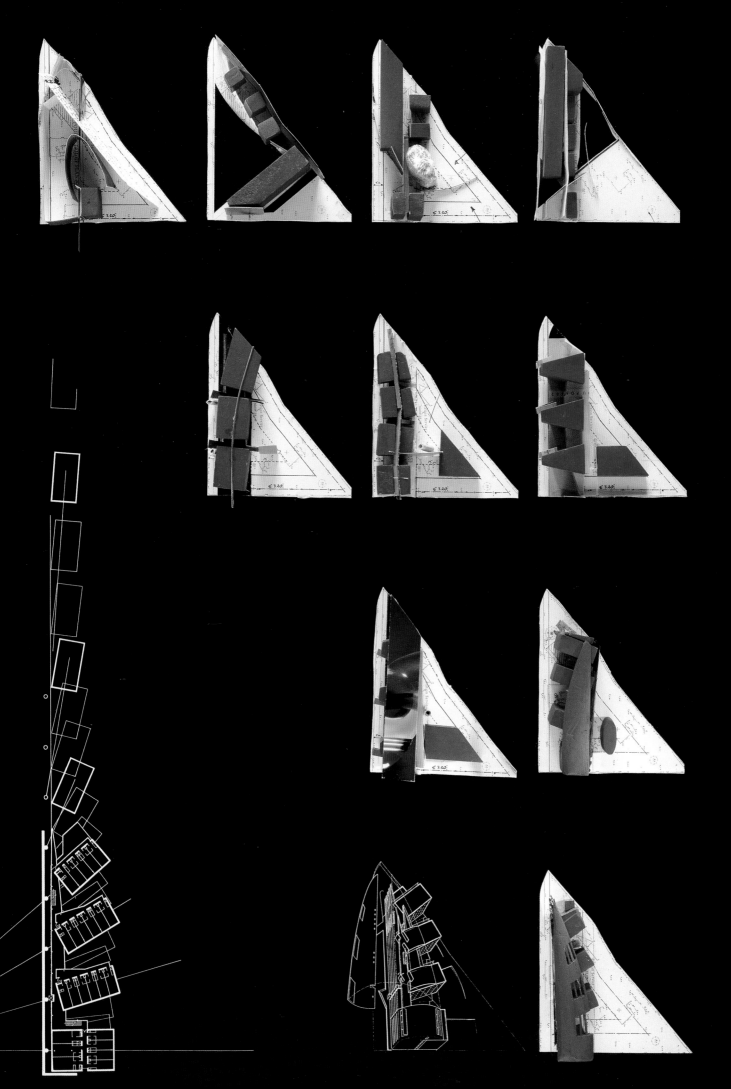

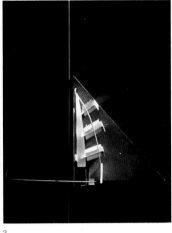

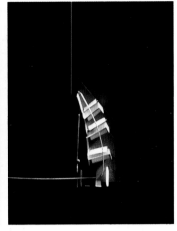

2

3

4

1 Models and drawings explore the different ways of breaking down the volume of the building and distributing it over the site.

2, 3, 4 Models demonstrate the play of rectilinear and curved geometries.

5, 6 Final scheme: massing plan (fig 5) and bird's-eye axonometric (fig 6) with the building's over-arching roof detached to reveal the interrelationship of the blocks and circulation spine.

Student Housing

Nantes

1991

This project, a student housing scheme in Nantes, is a further development of the idea of dissociation of functional elements, but here dissociation is deliberately given the appearance of unity in relation to the city by means of a homogeneous glass elevation on the city side which ties the separate elements together. Behind this screen, the building is broken down into four glass boxes, radiating out from the main horizontal circulation spine. The subdivision of the accommodation into blocks of six apartments on each of three levels was prompted by the programme, which

asked for a scheme in the style of a hotel so as to avoid the oppressive long corridors typical of most student hostels and other institutions. Each of the blocks is entered off an open balustrade running along the length of the garden facade of the main spine of the building, sheltered from the sky by an over-arching roof which springs from the top of the front facade and over the building like an umbrella.

The development is situated alongside a busy main road. The glass facade serves as a protective screen from the noise and fumes of passing traffic. But it also emphasizes the idea of horizontal movement through the building from one end to the other, while the subdivision of the building mass behind it forms a

rhythmic sequence of connected events marking out the route. The garden facade forms a gently curved trajectory in counterpoint to the rigid line of the front facade. The two meet at a point, forming a prow-like nose to the building at one end like a boat. This imagery is reinforced by the treatment of the semi open balustrades along the garden facade as deck-like walkways, although they could also be interpreted as cloisters.

The scheme represents a development of the ideas realized in the glass-fronted entrance hall of the BPO building, designed to create a promenade which extends the visual and physical limits of the building within the constraints of a relatively small surface area.

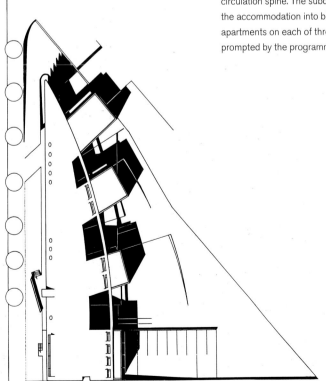

5

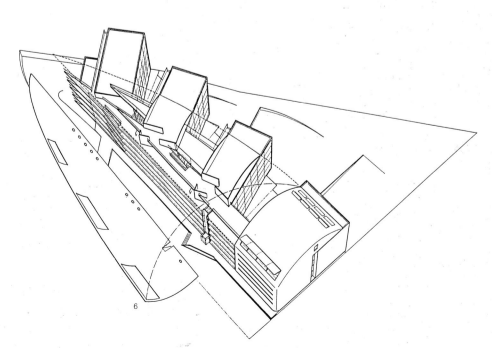

6

1

7

7 Bas-relief model
using different materials
to emphasize the
dissociation of volumes
unified under one roof.

8 Diagram clarifying
the overlaid geometries
of the scheme.

9 Models explore the
possible relationships
between the
accommodation blocks
anchored to the
circulation spine
along the road.

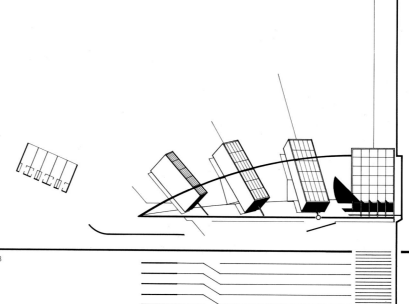

8

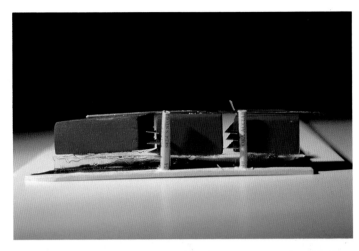

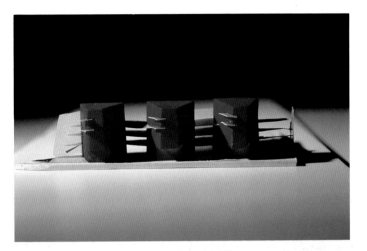

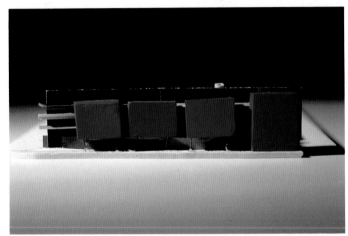

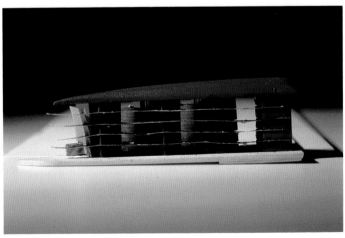

9

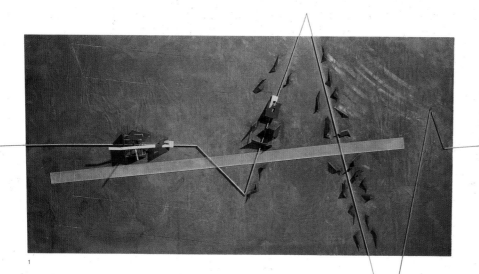

Un Signal

La Défense, Paris

1991

Every autumn, since 1989, France stages an 'Architecture Week' across the whole country designed to promote public awareness and knowledge of contemporary architecture and architects. Decq and Cornette's Signal was designed as a folly to be erected during Architecture Week (1–13 October) on a site at La Défense in front of the Grande Arche. Afterwards it was to be put to use as an information kiosk for the Public Office for the Development of La Défense ('EPAD') .

The intention behind the project was to illustrate the concept of architecture as process rather than monument. The construction consisted of a structural cube measuring one-tenth of the size of the cube of the Arche itself – each side being 120m square – clad with panels of metal and wood. The cube was to be reassembled and moved around on each of the seven days of the celebration week, each panel forming part of a

record of the daily events which would be completed on the last day. A cantilevered staircase was to pierce the cube diagonally, leading from ground level up to a viewing platform, suspended from a central mast, from which to contemplate the empty centre of the Arche.

The project was intended to express in a very concise shorthand form the ideas about occupation of space, marking of territory and visual sequence, which are central to Decq and Cornette's work. By setting the folly in front of the Arche they generated a relationship between the two very different structures – the arch so solid and monumental, the Signal lightweight and transitory – which was to have turned the whole square into a forcefield of energy crossed by a green laser beam directed from the Arc de Triomphe along the esplanade of La Défense and towards the Grande Arche, piercing it vertically. The scheme summed up a view of the city as a 'progressive layering, as a place of movement and time'.

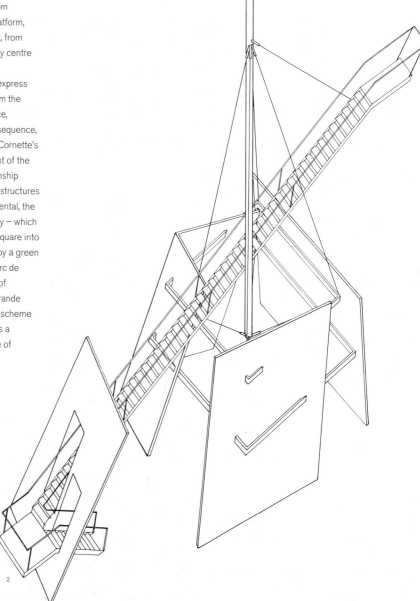

1 The model illustrates the process of construction over the period of 'Architecture Week,' while the zig-zag line indicates the course of a laser beam from the Arc de Triomphe to the Grande Arche, emphasizing the relationship between these two monuments. 2 The structure is based on the geometry of the cube, skewed and exploded. 3 Proposals for the stair and information screens.

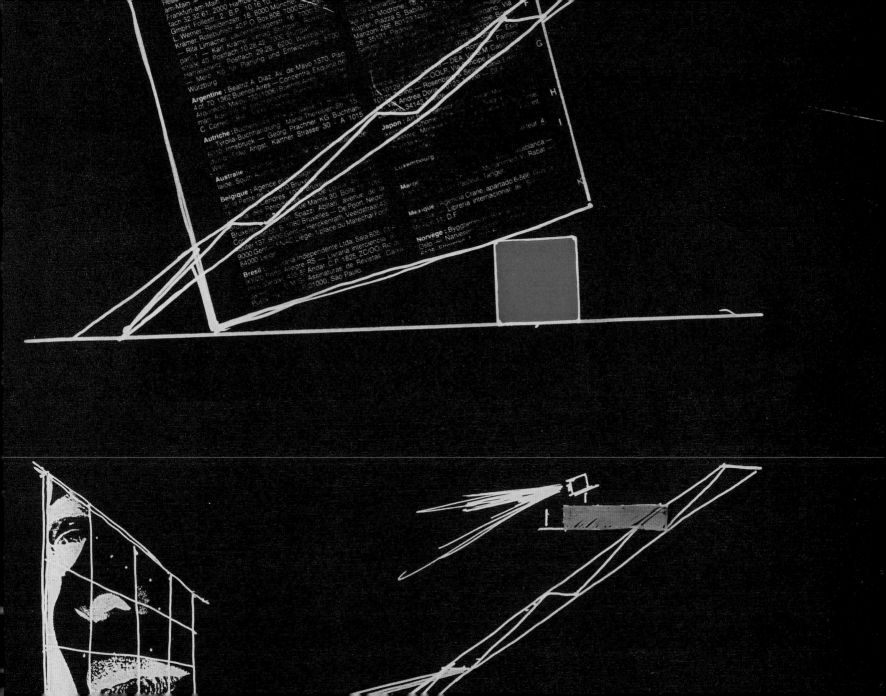

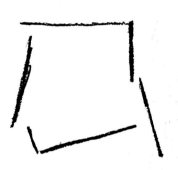

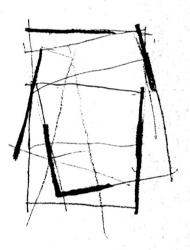

4, 5 A series of models and sketches exploring the different arrangements of structural elements and screens during the 'Architecture Week' event.

4

5

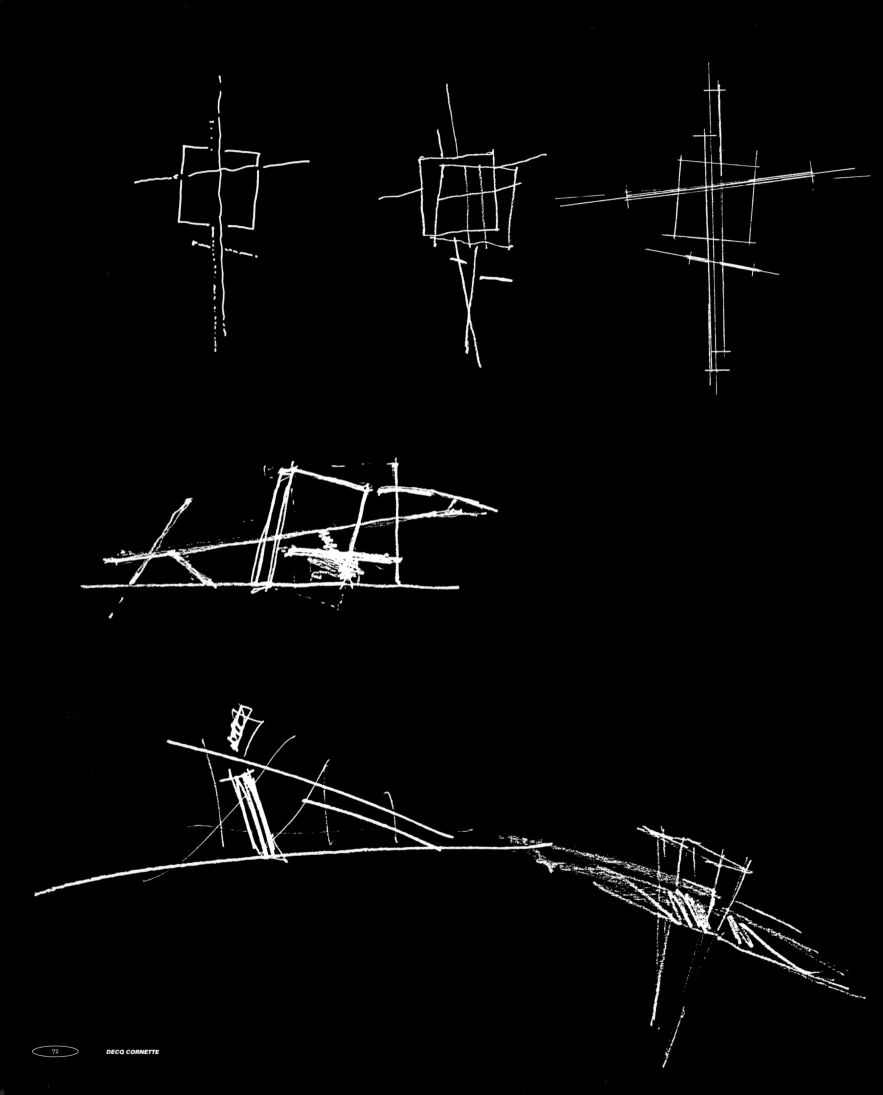

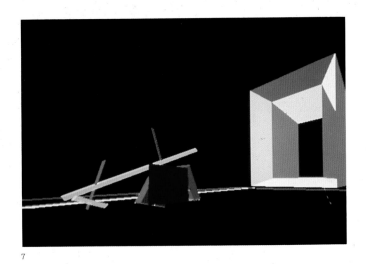

7

8

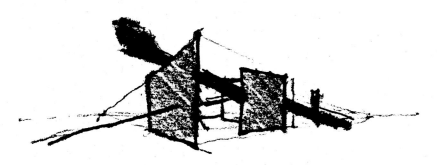

9

6   Sketch plans (above)
and profiles (centre and
below) of the proposed
installation.

7, 8, 9   Modelling of
the scheme showing its
relationship to the
Grande Arche.

10   East elevation.

11   South elevation.

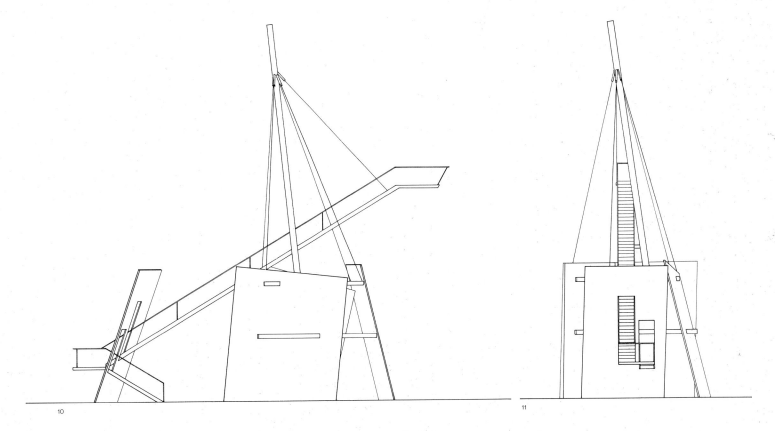

10

11

6

UN SIGNAL, LA DÉFENSE

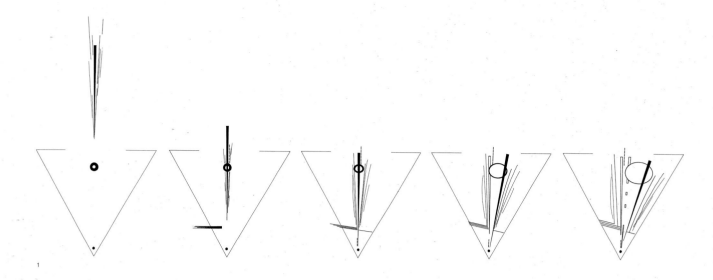

1

Centre for Cultural Exchange

Osaka, Japan

1991

This project explores the idea of: 'A progressive initiation into French culture. The promenade of successive spaces corresponds to the promenade through the world and the art of French living. The linear promenade around the hall expresses the amount of time necessary for the understanding of a long tradition.'

The brief was for a building that would serve as a cultural exchange centre for the twinned ports of Le Havre and Osaka. The main aim of the exercise was to introduce French wines to a Japanese public, but also the whole culture attached to wine production and consumption, and other products which pass through the port.

Two symbolic images generated the architectural form of the scheme.

The imagery of the ship, used in the plan, was intended to symbolize the passage between the ports of Le Hâvre and Osaka, its prow pointed towards the future. The imagery of the castle, used in the mass and elevations, was to represent the castles of the 'grands crus' in the wine growing countryside of France. Overall, the character of the project was intended to be futuristic but not high tech.

The project was designed immediately after the rue Manin housing scheme, taking the concept of the layered facade a stage further to structure the whole volume of the interior as a series of planes. The model constructed for the rue Manin scheme became an important design tool in the conception and development of the Osaka project, illustrating the continuity of ideas and methodology which underpins Decq and Cornette's working methods.

1 Series of diagrams illustrating the development of the proposal within the geometry of the site.
2 The model was developed directly from the rue Manin model showing the facade as layered planes. Here the entire volume of the building is broken down into a series of layers.
3 Diagrammatic drawings exploring the concept of layering and the relationship between volumes.
4 (overleaf) Detail of the model showing the intersection of vertical planes with the main drum-shaped volume of the scheme. From this angle the model evokes images of the castle: the social and administrative hub of the large French vineyards, transported to Osaka.

2

3

4 (pp 76–77)

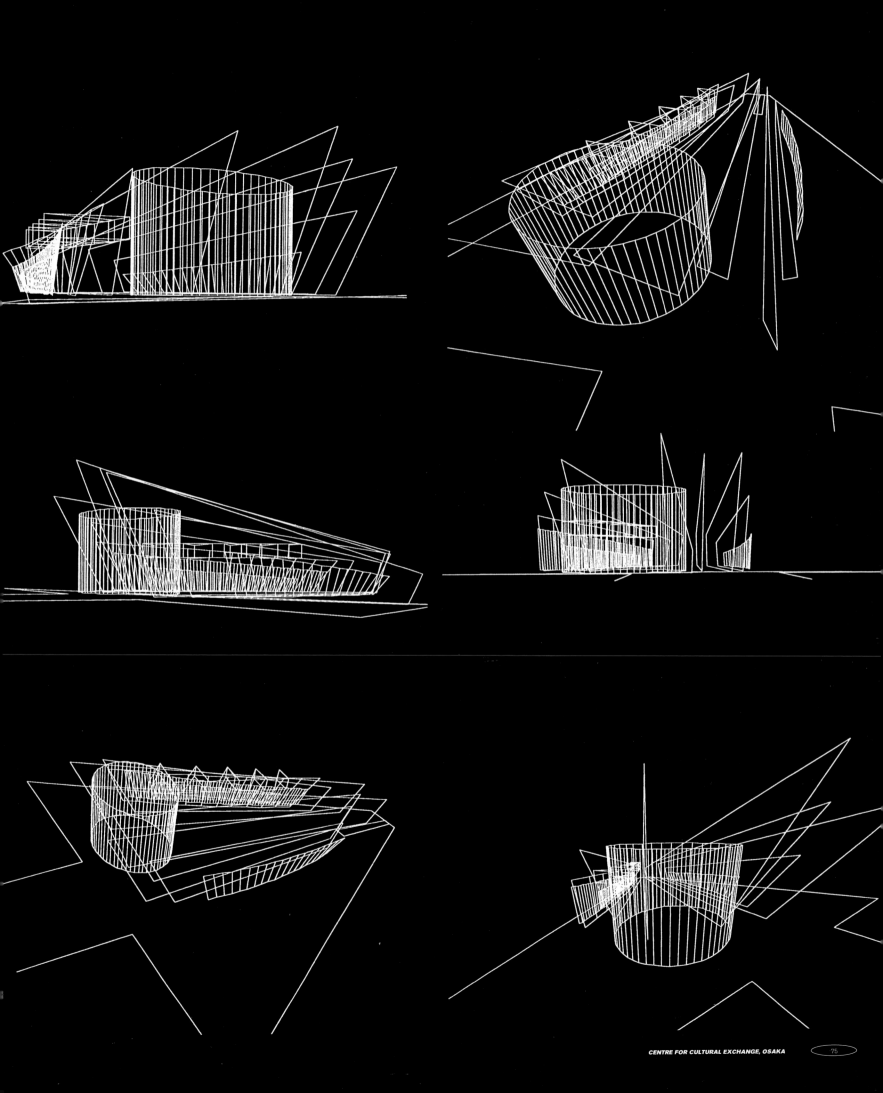

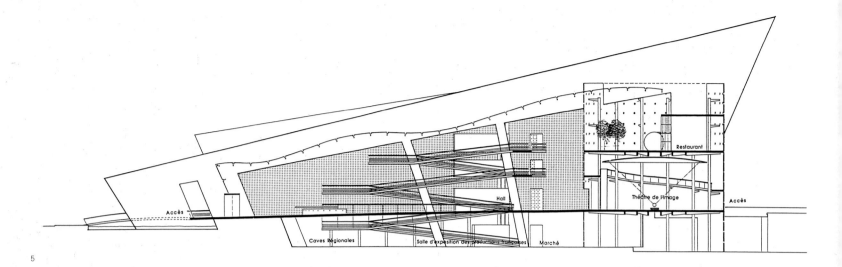

5

5   Section through
the building, showing the
linear promenade rising
vertically through the hall.
6   Second floor plan

showing the gallery
circulation looking down
into the void, and the
self-contained elliptical
space in the drum.

7, 8   Schematic drawings
highlighting the
interlocking and
dissociation of elements.

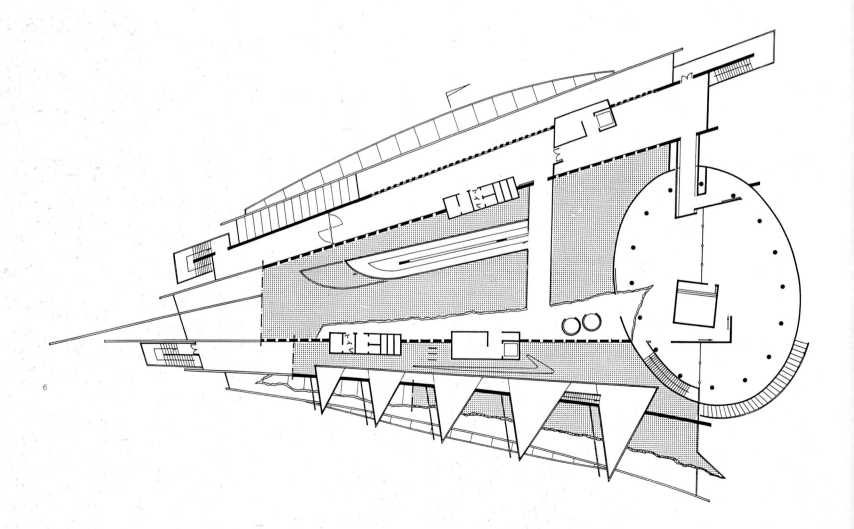

6

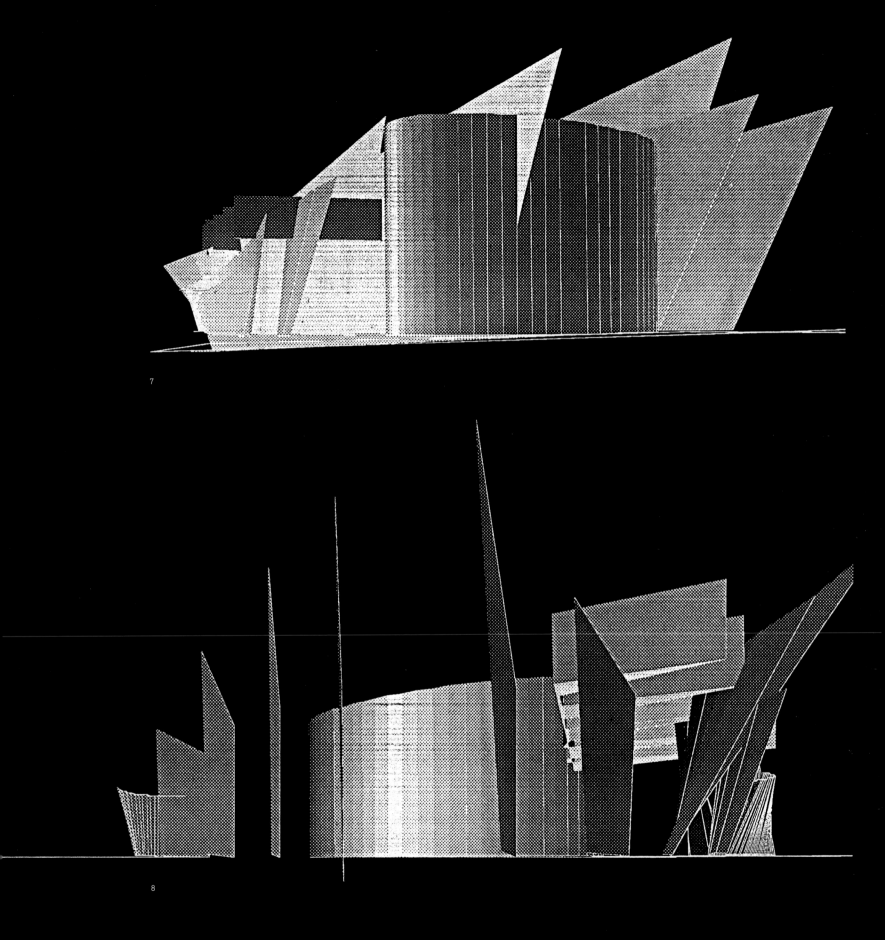

7

8

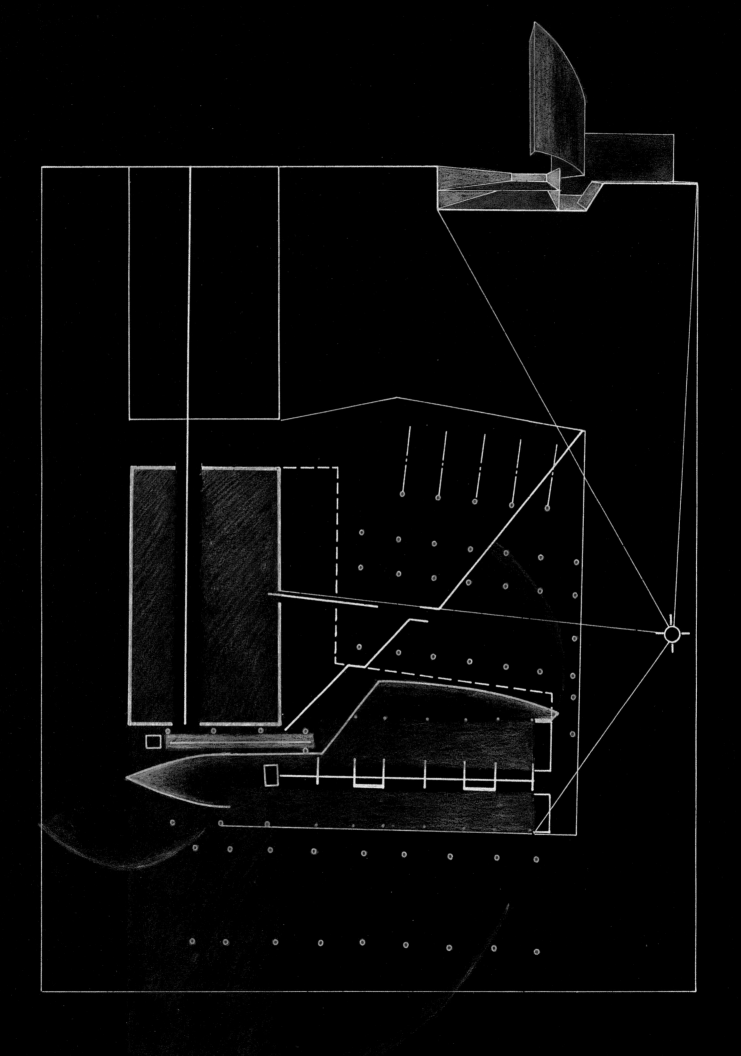

ENSAD 05 NOV 92

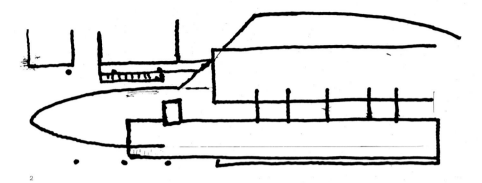

ENSAD – École Nationale Supérieure des Arts Décoratifs

Paris

1992

This project occupies a corner site in the historic centre of Paris, near the Panthéon. It involved the demolition and replacement of an existing structure on rue Erasme, slight restructuring of the main remaining building on rue Ulm, and more extensive restructuring of a smaller building between the two. The central issues were those of context, the relationship between the old and new buildings and approach to modification of existing buildings, and the treatment of an urban corner.

It was the treatment of this corner as, in medical terms, a 'fracture', which became the generating point of the scheme. The opening up of the structure articulates the relationship of the buildings on the site, forges a link between the city and the internal courtyard, and helps to reinforce, rather than disrupt, the continuity of the external facade of the school as it turns the corner, within the context of the historic urban fabric.

The facade of the replacement building on rue Erasme is conceived in homage to Jean Prouvé, who designed the panels of the original facade. The fragility of the existing foundations left little choice but to use a lightweight metal structure. The frame is clad in panels incorporating a system of movable aluminium shutters, modelled after the systems developed by Prouvé. The levels of the building were brought into line with those of the building on rue Ulm, in order to achieve fluid continuity of internal space throughout the school, and clear legibility of functions. The third building on the site, a small pavilion in the courtyard, is treated as an elemental object giving symbolic expression to its function as a computer science centre, located on the cross-axis of the geometries generated by the two main buildings.

1 Massing plan showing the main axes through the site and the distribution of the building around two sides to create an enclosed private precinct within.

2, 4 Diagrams delineating an aerial view of interlocking volumes of blocks on rue Erasme and the corner with rue Ulm.

3 Axonometric of the building on rue Erasme.

5 Collage showing perspective view of the segmented corner 'prow', forming an intersection point at the angle of the site.

5

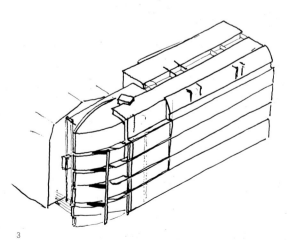

3

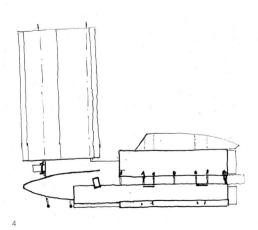

4

1

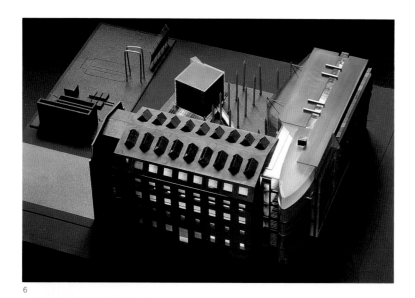

6

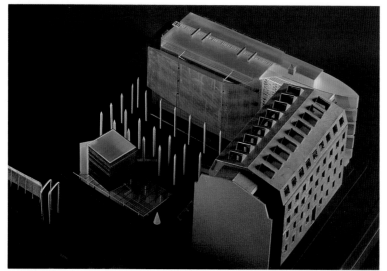

7

8

Views of the model:
6 Aerial view from the city side, showing a glimpse of the courtyard behind, with the computer science pavilion. The model of the old building is covered in lead, symbolizing the school's foundation. The model of the new building is a glass block, symbolizing its future. The old building contains administration, accommodation, library and meeting rooms; in the new block are the studios; and in the corner block are exhibition rooms.
7 View into the courtyard towards the rear elevation of the building on rue Erasme.
8 View into the courtyard towards the rear elevation of the building on rue Ulm.
9 Collage illustrating the continuity between the old and new blocks, broken at the corner like a broken arm. At this point, the structure and interior of the school is revealed.
10 Schematic diagrams illustrating the key concepts as separate stages in the design process.
11 (overleaf) View of the model from rue Erasme showing the corner intersection leading into the inner precinct.

9

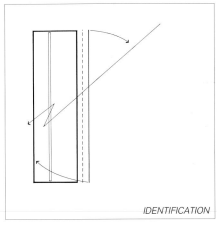

IDENTIFICATION

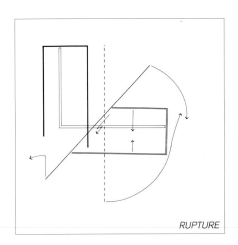

RUPTURE

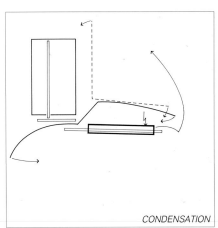

CONDENSATION

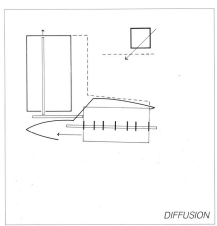

DIFFUSION

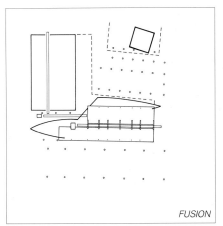

FUSION

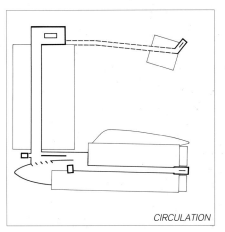

CIRCULATION

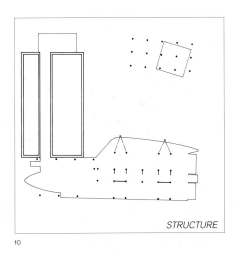

STRUCTURE

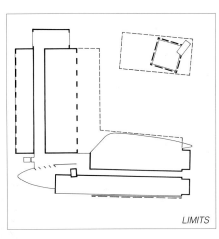

LIMITS

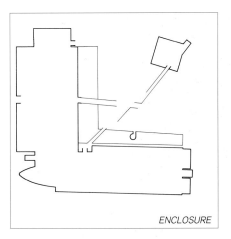

ENCLOSURE

10

11 (overleaf)

12 Perspective view of studios located at basement level.

13 Perspective view of computer science pavilion in the garden.

14 Perspective view showing the corner of the two streets.

15, 16 Sections through the existing building on rue Ulm and the courtyard, taken behind (fig 15) and in front of (fig 16) the computer science pavilion, showing the courtyard facade of the new building on rue Erasme.

12

13

14

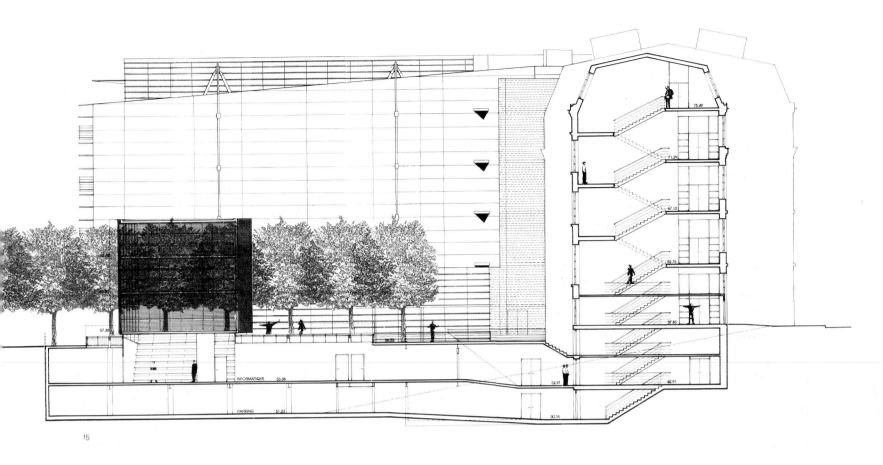

15

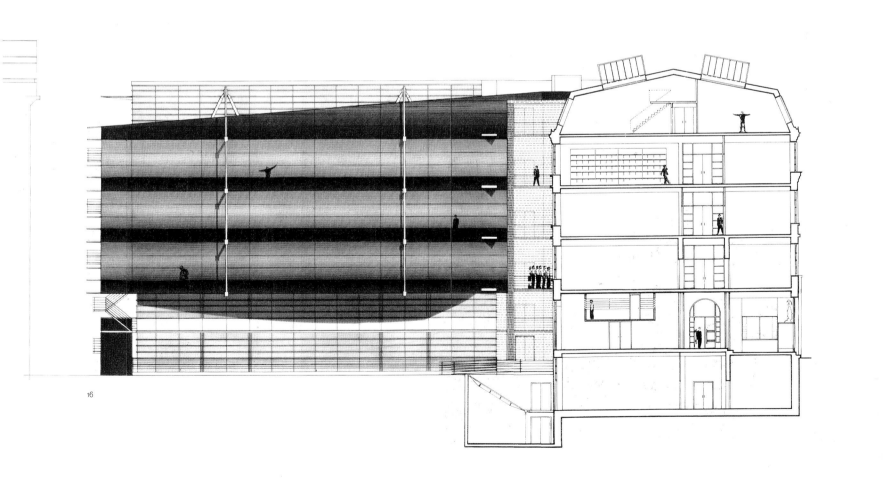

16

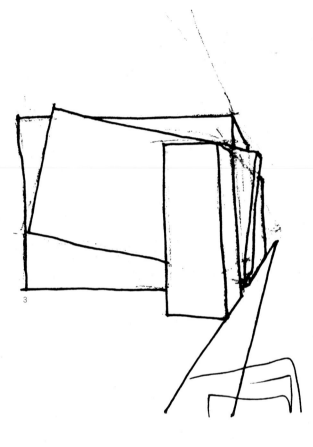

Social Housing

Rue Ernestine, Paris

1992–95

This new housing block in the working-class, predominantly ethnic Goutte d'Or neighbourhood of Paris, was designed to make the most of a narrow site with a very small street frontage. The result is a rather elegant, metal-clad building, entirely rectilinear in its outward profile and quite cool compared to much of Decq and Cornette's other work, providing eleven very generously sized apartments which enjoy high levels of natural light and views out.

The plan is T-shaped, with the short arm across the front of the site containing the staircase and lift giving access to walkways above. The walkways, from ground to top floor, are incorporated within a narrow strip along the edge of the long arm of the T, stretching back into the site. The entrances to the flats are ranged off them, each flat occupying the width of the block, with views out into a small courtyard on the other side. Balconies on the street frontage help to animate the external facade.

The apartments are duplexes (maisonettes), with double-height glazed frontages on the courtyard side. They are fitted out to a high standard, with timber flooring and metal balustrades, partly to compensate for the area – although the budget was only that of a mid-range housing scheme. The communal areas are also carefully thought out in order to maximize the pleasure of living in the building. The lift is glazed, allowing views out into the very narrow internal courtyard, floored in ships timbers, which separates the building from its neighbours on that side. The staircase is shielded from the street behind a perforated screen, providing privacy while also allowing views out into the street.

The entrance hall is animated by a shallow curved seating area recessed beneath the walkway above and made to appear double its length by means of a mirror: an interaction of straight and curved lines which vividly recalls the design of the hall at the BPO's Administrative Centre. A blue column rises up through the vertical space, marking the location of the stair.

1 View along the upper level walkway past the main access stair and the blue painted column rising up through the space from the entrance lobby.

2 Computer image of the front elevation, revealing the scale of the building in relation to its neighbours, and its horizontal and vertical articulation.

3, 4 Sketches show how the different volumes interlock to form a whole.

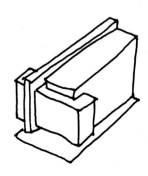

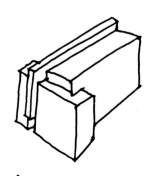

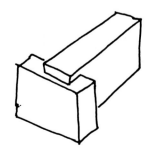

4

5

DECQ CORNETTE

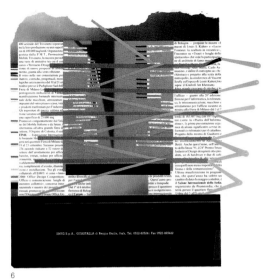

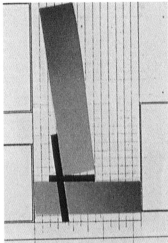

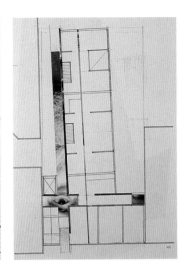

6

5 View of the rear and
side elevation across
the courtyard. The
double-height glazed
sections of the facade
allow plentiful natural
light to enter the flats,
and good views out.
6 Series of drawings

exploring different ways
of siting the building.
7 Conceptual studies.
8 Massing plan of
the building, showing
its relationship with
its neighbours and
the street.

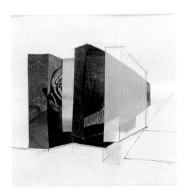

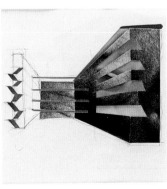

7

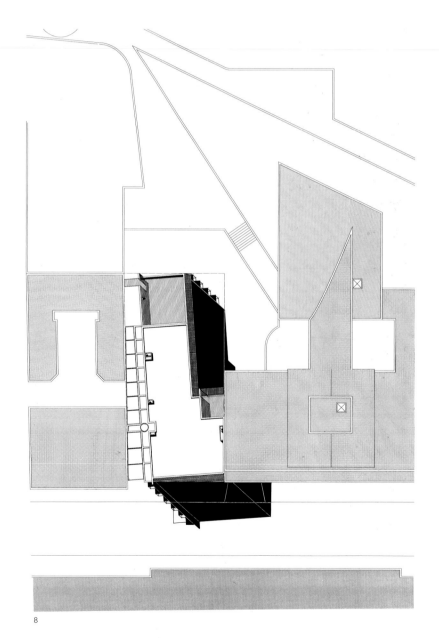

8

SOCIAL HOUSING, RUE ERNESTINE

9

9 Study sketches illustrating the corner of the two volumes at the internal courtyard.

10 View along the balcony walkways on the open side of the building.

11 View from the staircase through the glazed elevation and onto the street.

12 View through the narrow courtyard slot between Decq and Cornette's building and its immediate neighbour on the left.

10

11

12

13

14

15

16

13, 14, 15, 16 Interior views of apartments. Natural timber floors and clean metal detailing maximize the sense of space and light.

17, 18, 19 Floor plans (from left to right):

ground, first and top floor. The apartments are planned to be as open as possible.

20 View through the entrance hall, with its concave seating recess and mirror-glass rear wall.

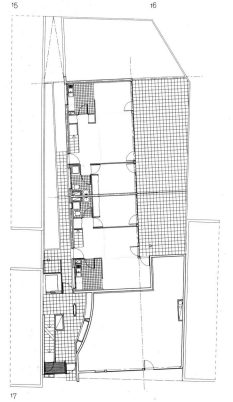
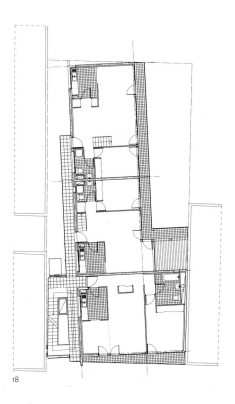
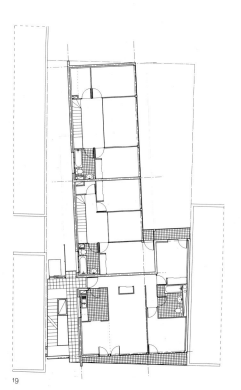

17

18

19

20

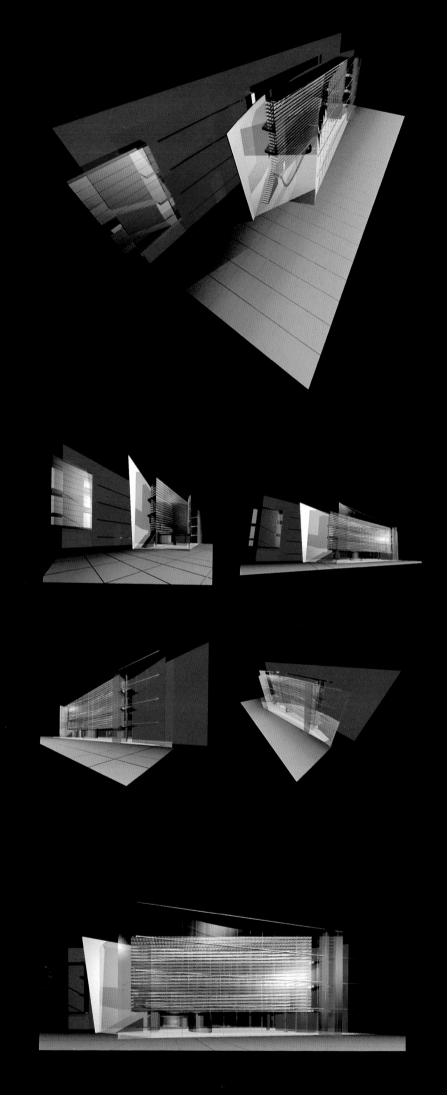

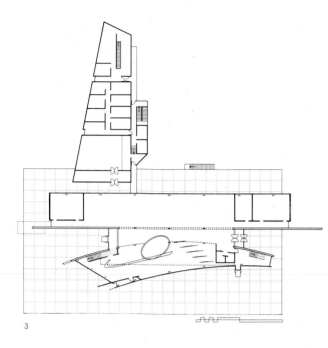

3

2

4

Banque de France

Montpellier

1993

The site for this project was a wooded slope on the approaches to Montpellier town centre. The brief asked for a building consisting of three different elements: a branch office [succursale], strongroom [caisse institutionelle], and social centre. The scheme was conceived in the spirit of the BPO, with which it has much in common in terms of programme, and there are strong similarities in the design. The core of the plan is a rectangular box containing the office areas, with an arc-shaped public zone pulled out and detached from it in front, in much the same manner as the public hall of the BPO.

The positioning of the building on the site is treated in the manner of the 'hôtel particulier', or traditional grand French private residence, in its grounds. The different functions are gathered together in one fairly compact building in order to leave as much of the rest of the site as clear as possible, and maintain the character of a garden around the social

centre, which sits behind and at right angles to the rectangular core of the plan. The treatment of the entry and public hall of the building is designed to recall the traditional 'Cour d'Honneur' (court of honour) of the 'hôtel particulier'.

Although the proposed building is a homogeneous architectural entity, it is broken down in plan and volume, to give each of the three distinct elements specified by the programme its own identity. The internal space is interpreted, and held together, as a series of numerous thresholds implying a constant level of exchange between different parties within the building. The branch office, consisting of the rectangular and curved blocks comprising the main building mass, is conceived as a series of vertical plans, or layering of transparent curved and straight planes. The curved block, containing the public space, is intended to give expression to the identity and image of the bank; the rectangular block, containing the offices, is a more ordinary building, designed for easy modification in the future according to the bank's needs. The two are detached from each other,

1 Computer images exploring the layered structure of the building from the front facade, through the public entrance hall and atrium, to the private domain of the offices in the main block behind.

2 Sketch showing the intermediary space between the public entrance hall and

the main volume of the branch office behind.

3 Ground plan of the building and gridded forecourt.

4 Massing plan of the building on site, showing the dissociation of elements.

5 Coloured concept sketches.

5

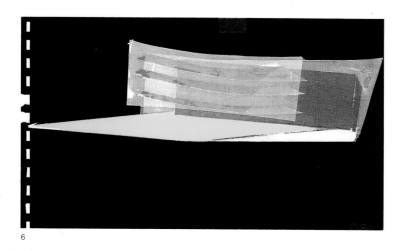

6

6 Collage exploring the relationship of the various elements.
7 Bird's-eye axonometric showing the location of services in the public zone to the fore of the main block.
8 Sketch perspective of the front of the building, describing its curving embrace around the forecourt.
9 View of model from the front forecourt, with the social centre visible behind sloping downhill away from the main building.

but connected by an atrium which forms a transitional space between the public and private areas.

The strongroom and associated offices are treated as an armoured bunker located below ground, underneath the building and its forecourt, which is slightly elevated to allow light to enter the basement spaces. The gap between ground and forecourt level widens at the back of the building, as the ground slopes away downhill, allowing the basement spaces to open up to the garden to a certain extent. The two-storey social centre is set behind and beneath the building following the downhill slope. The roof is shaped as a series of waves emphasizing the slope of the land. It shelters three entities contained inside: the conference room, the cafeteria, and the trade union premises.

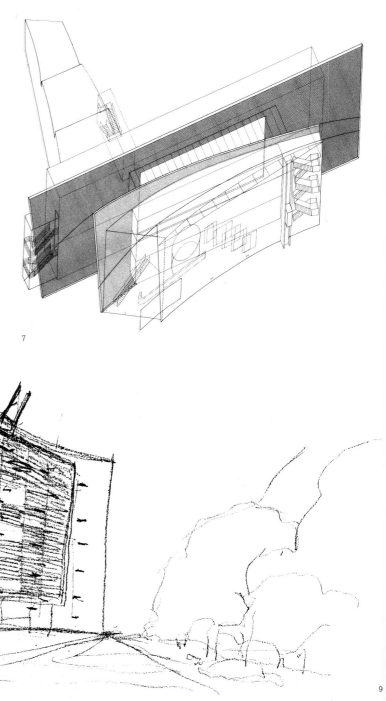

7

8

9

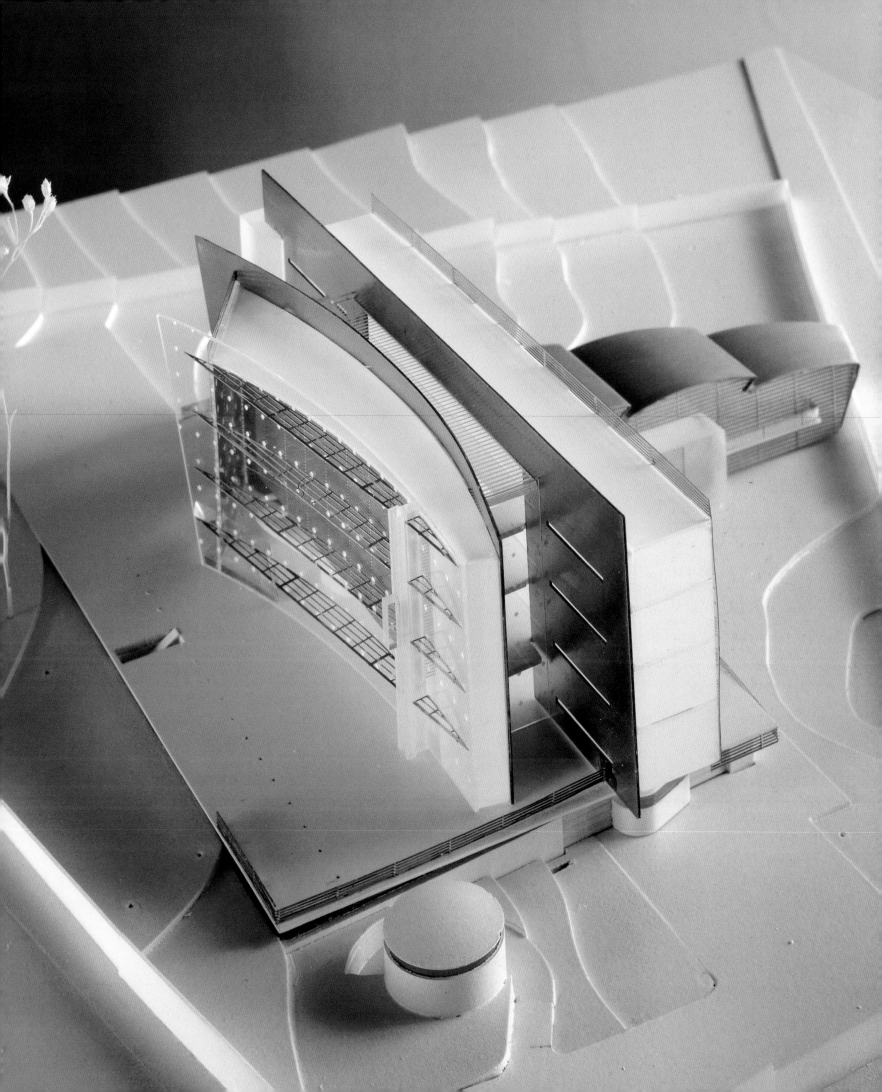

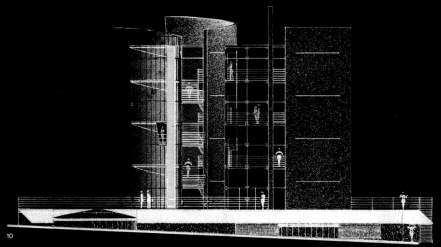

10

10 East elevation: staff entrance.

11 Cross section through the building.

12 West elevation: public entrance.

13 Elevation of the main block, showing the continuity of horizontal circulation.

14, 15 Views of the model from the

side and front.

16 Elevation of the public entrance hall, with the profile of the main block visible behind.

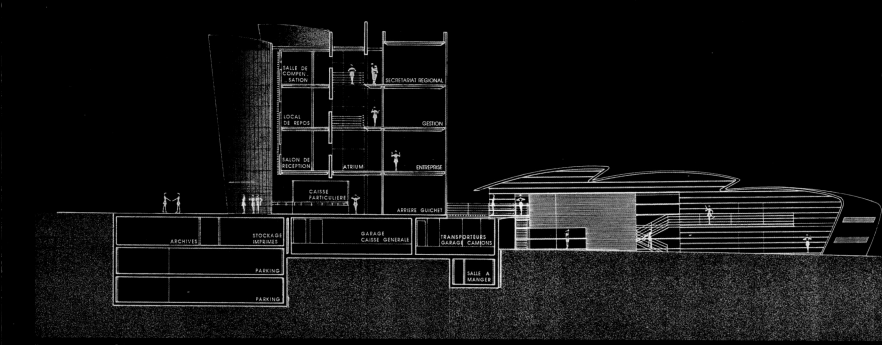

SALLE DE COMPEN- SATION

SECRETARIAT REGIONAL

LOCAL DE REPOS

GESTION

SALON DE RECEPTION

ATRIUM

ENTREPRISE

CAISSE PARTICULIERE

ARRIERE GUICHET

ARCHIVES

STOCKAGE IMPRIMES

GARAGE CAISSE GENERALE

TRANSPORTEURS GARAGE CAMIONS

SALLE A MANGER

PARKING

PARKING

11

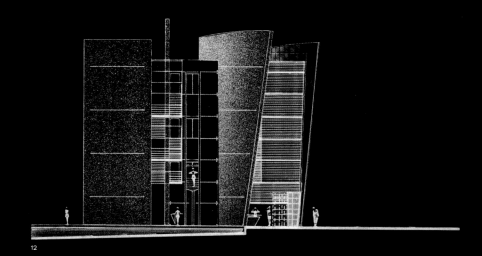

12

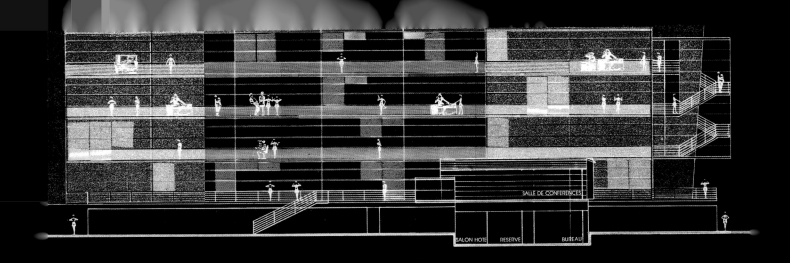

SALLE DE CONFÉRENCES

SALON HOTE   RESERVE   BUREAU

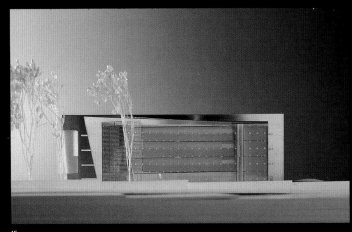

15

1

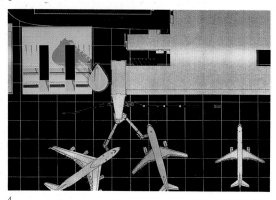

2

Bordeaux-Mérignac Airport

Control Tower and Technical Building

Bordeaux-Mérignac

1993

The scheme is generated by the dynamic tension between the vertical element of the tower and the ground-hugging horizontal element of the technical block. The simplicity of the linear overall layout was intended to compensate for the complexity of the programme, and also to suggest a streamlined, high-performance image evocative of aeronautic engineering. The low-lying main block has a gently curved roof which is lower at the back than at the front, so that in section and profile it resembles the nose of a plane or train. The plan is E-shaped, allowing each section a degree of autonomy, connected by common circulation and meeting areas. The long facade is orientated towards the city to present a clear image of the building as a homogeneous entity. The control tower is detached from the main building, standing close to it at one end. Its oval-shaped base and head contrast with the linearity of the technical block.

The proposed structure of the building is mainly metal, fabricated by industrial production methods, for reasons of precision, modular flexibility, speed of execution, and to achieve a lightweight, streamlined appearance – especially for the tower, a tripod-like structure which was to be as light as possible. The base is of concrete, as is that of the technical block, in order to provide more solid accommodation for storage areas, shops, and heavy-duty workshops, as well as to give some protection to the facades from traffic around the building. In the end, however, the client was worried by the high level of transparency in the building for reasons of security.

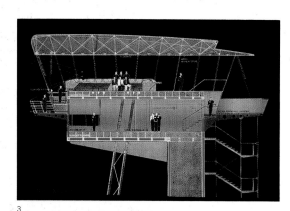

3

1 Inspirational image of 1930's wind generator for the design of the control tower.
2 Cross section through the control tower and technical building.
3 Cross section throught the top of the control tower.
4 Aerial view showing the scale of the building in relation to the planes.
5 Early sketch of the control tower.
6 Worm's-eye view of the control tower, revealing the stair and underside of head. The vertical tower contrasts with the emphatic horizontality of the technical building.
7 (overleaf) Computer-generated perspective of the technical building and tower.

4

5

6

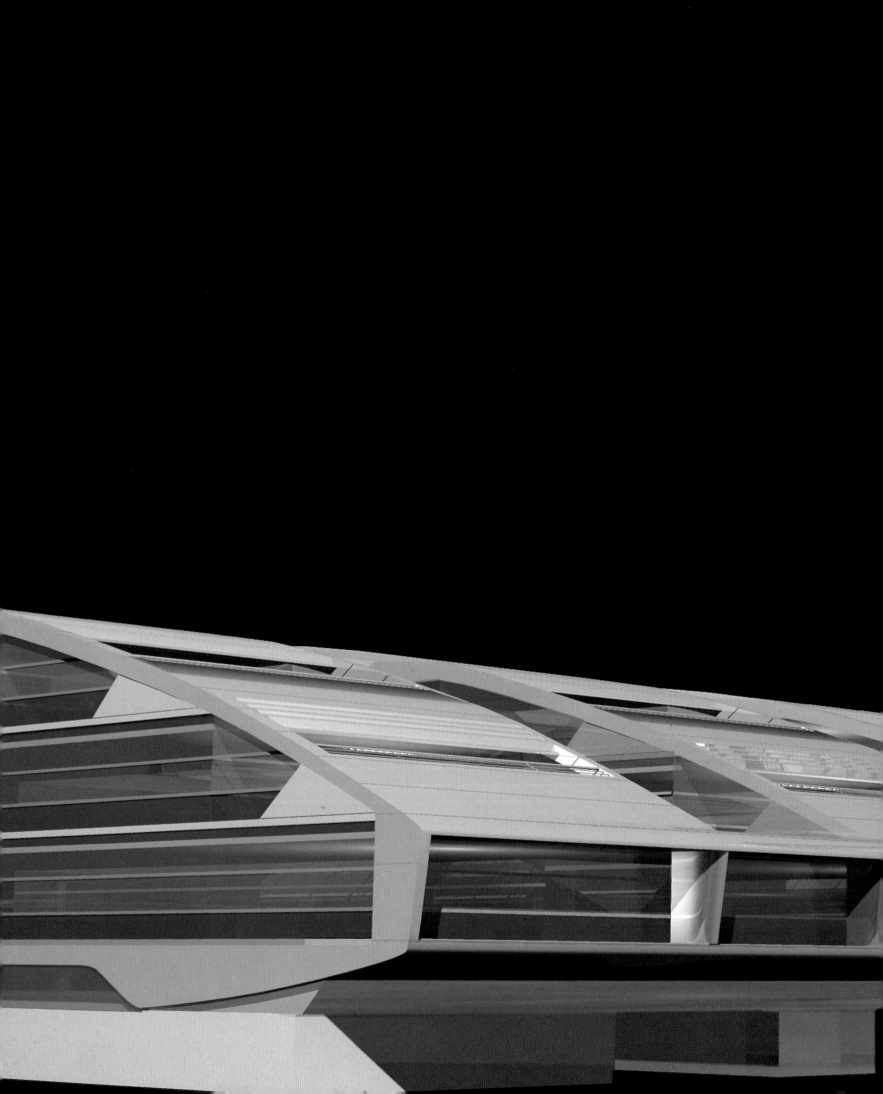

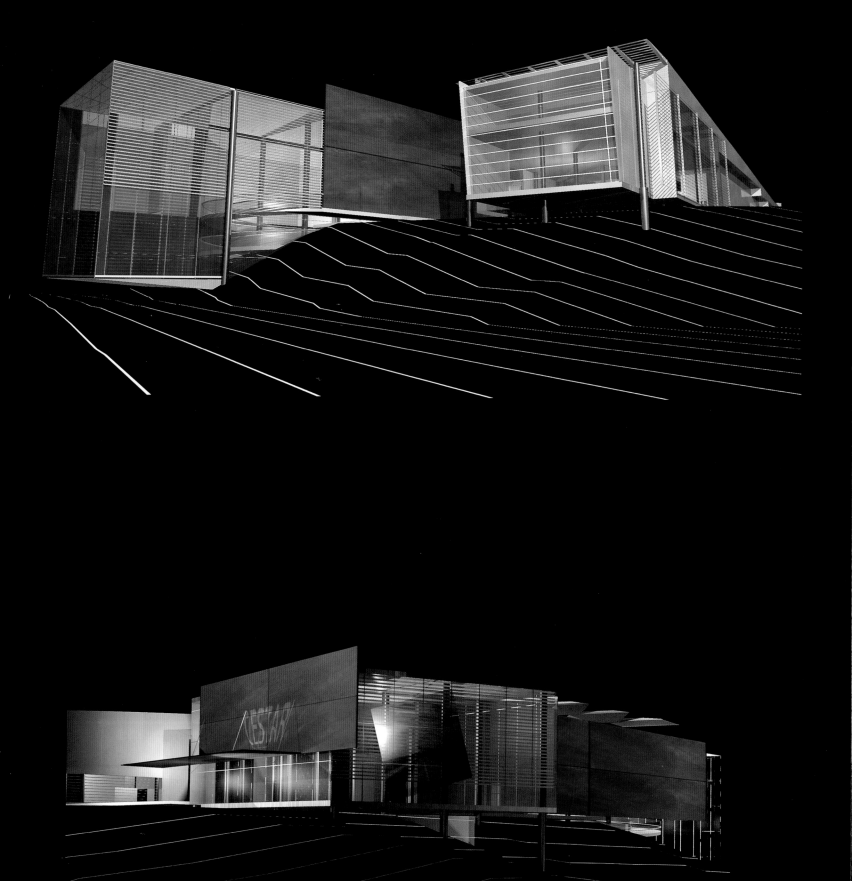

1 Computer image showing the scheme broken down into two volumes, seen from the rear, one containing the exhibition spaces and the other the back-up and resource facilities.

2 Computer image of the entrance facade and canopy, opening into the exhibition spaces, with the curved facade of the support building seen behind.

3 Sketch view from the road.

4 Diagrams of the exhibition space's internal organization conceived as different chains of relationships.

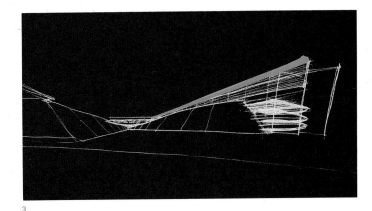

3

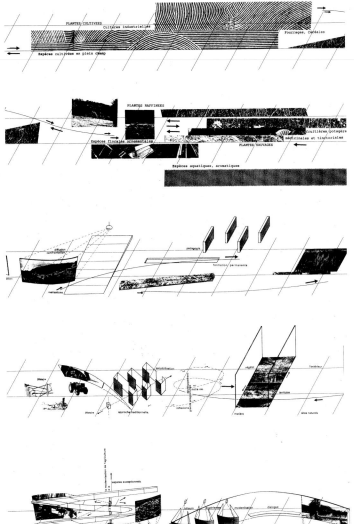

1

4

CESTAR – Centre d'Études Scientifiques des Techniques Agricoles et Rurales

Arras

1993

Once again, the concepts of dissociation and fragmentation are given very clear expression in this project for a museum of agriculture in the countryside outside the town of Arras. The building is broken down into two rectangular volumes, one containing the exhibition spaces and the other back-up and resource facilities, including a cafeteria. This mode of organization reflects the different criteria relating to the various activities for heating, security and even hours of opening, allowing the two parts of the building a degree of autonomy and independence from each other. The planning was also designed to reflect the idea of a production line, forging a connection between the culture of agriculture and industry, but as a complex chain of relationships rather than a simple linear progression.

The two volumes are connected by a glazed atrium opening directly into the exhibition areas on one side, and into the curved circulation spine of the support building on the other. The entrance opens into the atrium between the buildings, orientated towards the road. The inner facade of the support building projects out beyond it, curving away revealingly. The entrance is slightly elevated above ground level, reached by a gently sloping ramp, which can also be read as a strip of wheat penetrating the interior. This has the important effect of detaching the building from the ground, so that it appears to be floating just above it, as well as allowing light to filter down into the lower ground floor spaces. The atrium widens towards the garden side, as the two buildings, aligned on different axes, part slightly. The use of a central atrium focuses movement through the core, filtering out to either side, and allows circulation space in the rest of the building to be reduced to a minimum. It creates a fluid indoor/outdoor space between the main structural volumes.

The building is constructed out of glass and metal, clad in floating steel panels which reveal wide expanses of glass. It has a high degree of transparency, exposing the contents on display inside, and forging a link between the interior and the river and working gardens, growing different crops and vegetables, onto which the building looks and which form an integral part of the museum's display. The building was designed to act as an interface, like a camera lens, between nature at first hand and nature as represented by the exhibition material. On the other side, it confronts the main highway, forming a highly visible landmark at the entrance to the town.

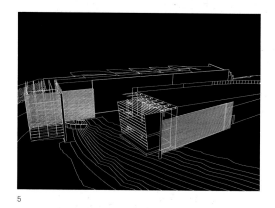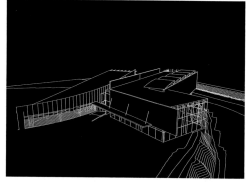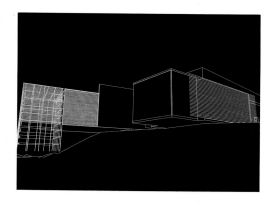

5

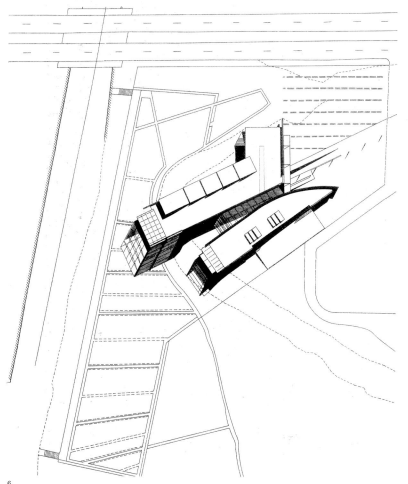

6

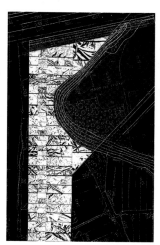

7

5 Axonometrics viewed from the gardens (left and right) and the entrance elevation (centre).
6 Massing plan of the building on site, revealing the engagement between architecture and the garden, where examples of regional agriculture are exhibited.
7 Collages exploring the layout of the landscape.
8 Aerial view of the model highlighting the transparency of the blocks towards the gardens and river.

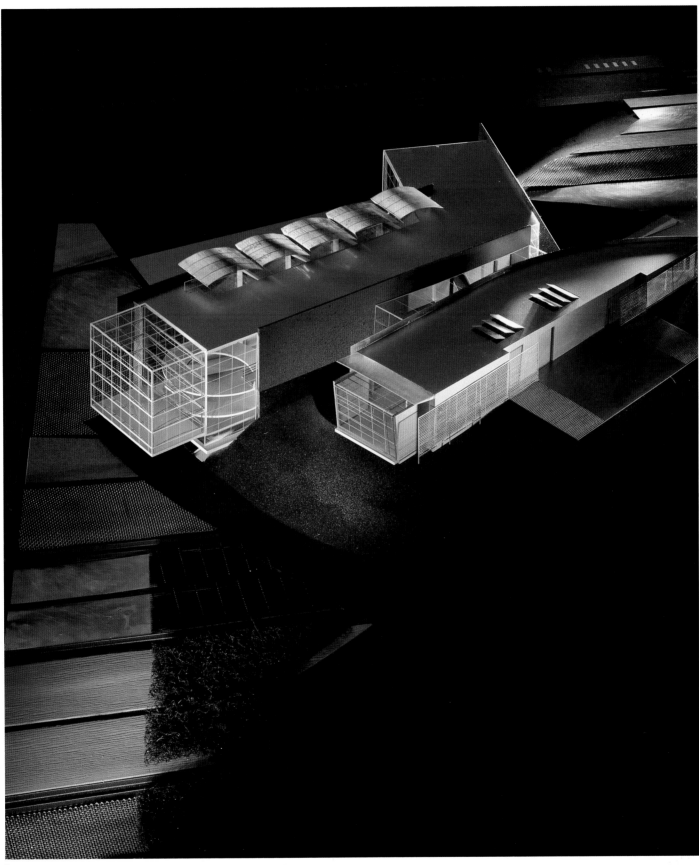

8

9

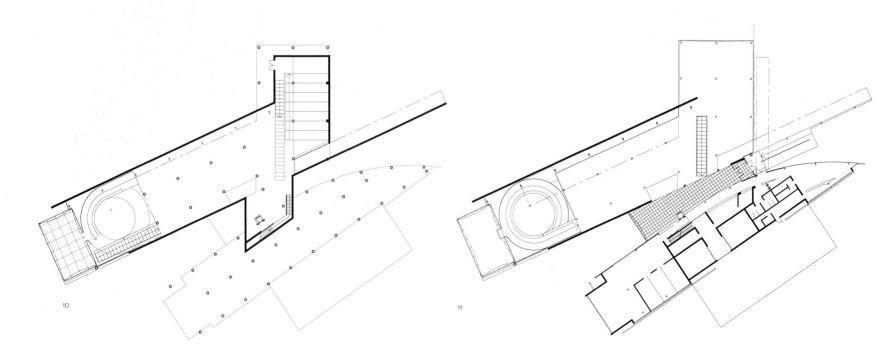

10

11

DECQ CORNETTE

9 Sketch perspective view of the opening between the buildings with the exhibition material visible through the transparent facade to the right.

10 Basement level plan of the exhibition block.

11 Ground floor plan.

12, 13, 14, 15, 16 Images of the interior exhibition space (figs 12, 13, 14, 16) and vertical circulation ramp at the far end of the exhibition block looking out onto the gardens (fig 15).

15

12

13

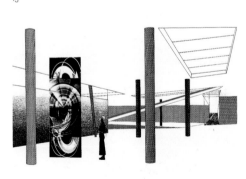

14

16

2

1 Aerial view of the
project, revealing
the relationship
between the museum
and the town.
2 Image showing the
planes on display in the
'glass aeroplane wing'

projecting out onto the
runway.
3 View of the existing
hangars.
4 Interior view through
the 'glass aeroplane
wing', located in front of
the former terminal.

Air and Space Museum

Le Bourget

1993

Le Bourget is Paris' oldest airport, now used only for freight, for a biannual aeronautic trade fair, and as a museum of planes and equipment haphazardly housed in the old hangars on the site. The client wanted a vision of what the museum might be. Decq and Cornette produced a scheme aimed at stimulating the imagination, rather than saturating the visitor with educational material, by presenting the objects as 'splendid pieces of industrial design and high technology, as machines of adventure and dreams'.

To this end it was important to incorporate a sense of movement and speed into the scheme. It consists of an 800m-long axis, or vertebral column, connecting a linear series of exhibition spaces extending to either side of a central, two-storey core – the old airport building itself – looking out over the runway at the back, and onto a wide forecourt at the front. A travelator runs the length of the axis, allowing visitors to make a rapid promenade through the entire exhibition before focusing on particular areas of interest. The core area contains contextual and educational material encompassing film, video, photographs, models and interactive booths. This secondary material is deliberately dissociated from the exhibition objects themselves, the planes displayed in the existing hangars along one side of the axis, and in the new glass display area on the other side, projecting out onto the forecourt or runway. This 'glass aeroplane wing', so-called on account of its aerodynamic shape, forms an interface between the museum and the runway.

3

4

1

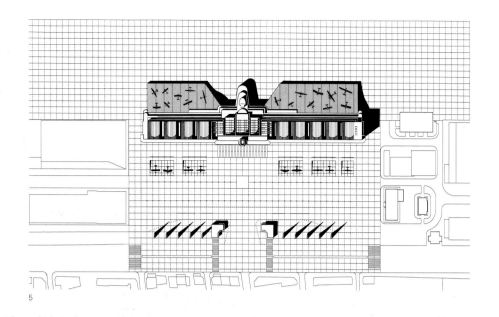

5

5 Site plan of the
building with the new
transparent extensions
along its length.

6, 7 Perspective views
across the the entrance
court., showing (fig 7)
the 'vitrines' for the
planes excavated into
the ground.

8 Cross section
through the exhibition
display in the new
transparent wing.

9, 10, 11 Images of the
exhibition display,
emphasizing its
dynamic, kinetic quality.

6

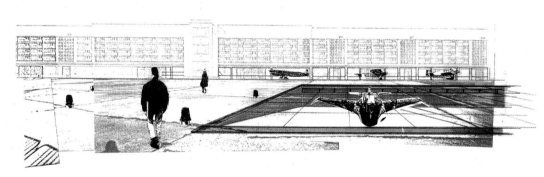

7

L'AILE DE VERRE   LE NOYAU LINÉAIRE   LA GALERIE

8

LE TRANSBORDEUR   LE NOYAU LINEAIRE   L'AILE-AUVENT

9

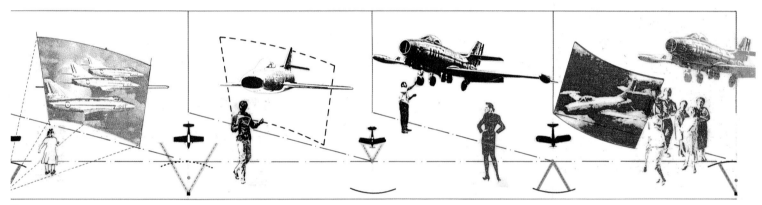

10

11

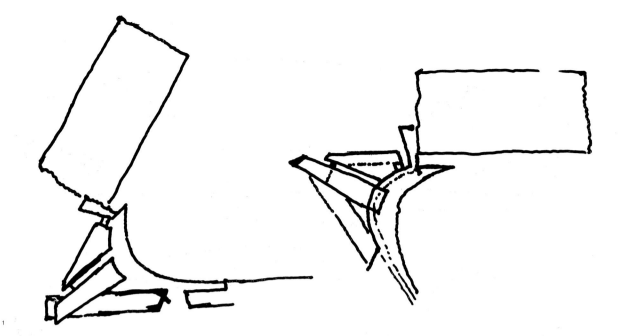

Lycée Alfred Nobel

Clichy-sous-Bois

1993

There are strong similarities between this scheme for a semi-vocational, semi-academic educational institution, and ENSAD, notably in the handling of the corner. The classrooms and workshops are separated into two main buildings treated as walls delineating the boundaries of the site, and set at an acute angle to each other, like 'a pair of open arms', or the fractured arm used as an analogy in the ENSAD design.

The joint between the two is articulated by a third building containing the main

hall, library and administrative accommodation. This building is itself articulated as an ensemble of different volumes giving expression to the different functions. The sculptural treatment contrasts with the flat smooth exteriors of the blocks either side. It opens a passage into the enclosed interior of the site, which is interpreted as a sheltered, almost cloistered garden opening out towards the east.

A freestanding, ovoid-shaped restaurant is located within the grounds, its curved lines hinting playfully at the symbolism of a spaceship unexpectedly landed on the site, and contrasting with the angularity of the rest of the complex.

The different functions of the main buildings are reflected in the choice of materials for the facades. The classroom and administrative blocks are clad in prefabricated concrete panels, the workshop block in metal panels. The imagery of the building, with its curved metal roofs, comes from the world of industrial design rather than architecture: streamlined, high-tech forms suggestive of the latest models in the motor or locomotive industries, designed to move at high speed, merely skimming the ground.

3

1, 2, 3 Sketch diagrams and the model show the development of the angle between the two buildings.

4 Sketches of the ovoid building housing the restaurant: it is inspired by the front of a classic car, the Chrysler Dodge Viper.

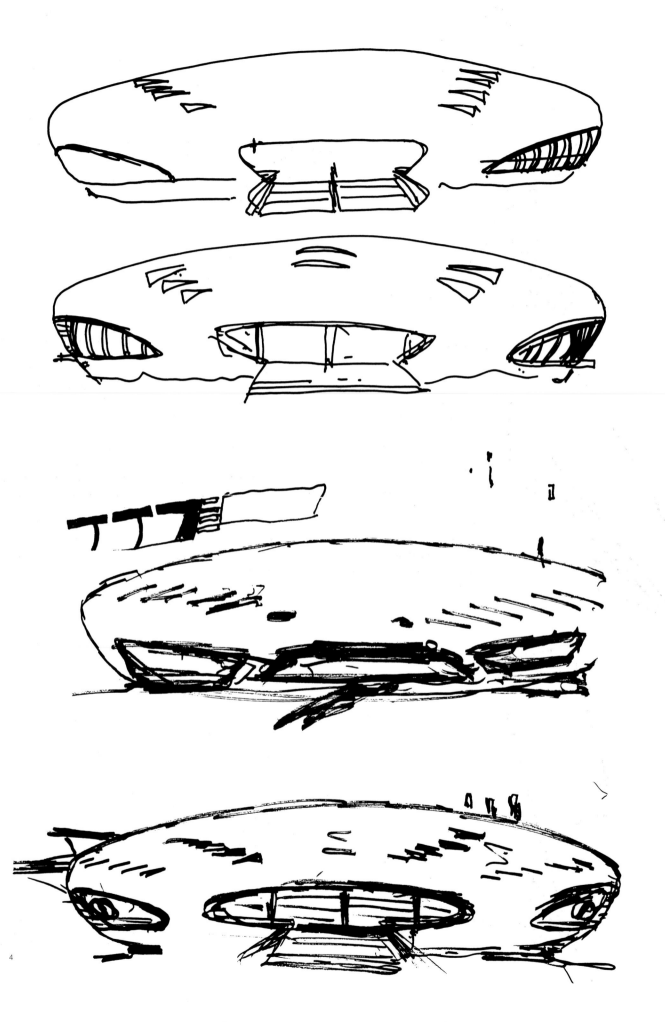

5 The angle between
the buildings is handled
as a collection of
smaller interlocking
elements, each
containing different
functions: offices,
library, lecture room,
social centre, etc.
6 Site and ground floor
plan. As at ENSAD, the
building forms an
enclosure around a
private inner court.
7, 8 Section through
the main administrative
block at an angle (fig 7)
and elevation (fig 8).

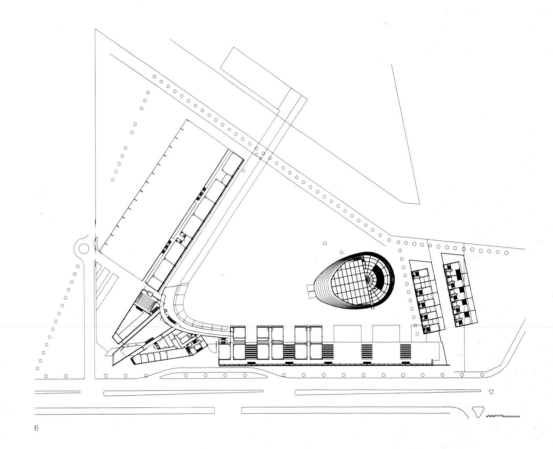

6

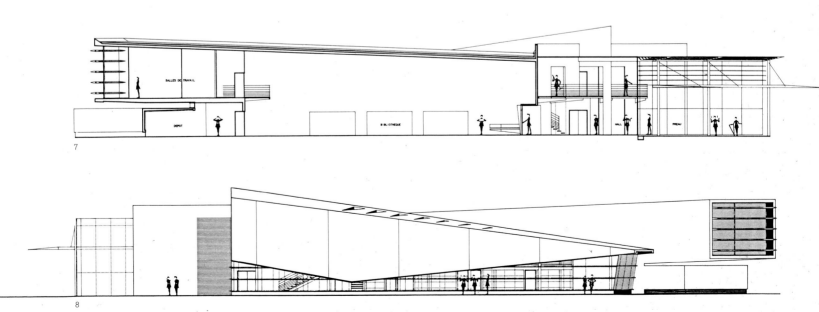

7

8

LYCÉE ALFRED NOBEL

5

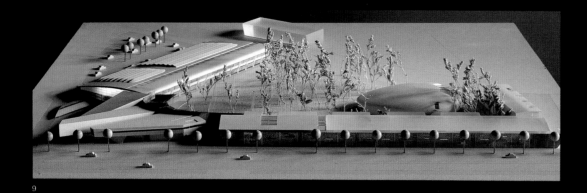

9

10

9   Aerial view of the
model revealing the
private precinct within.
10, 11   Elevation and
computer image of the
new corner block.
12   Elevations and
sections through the
restaurant block.

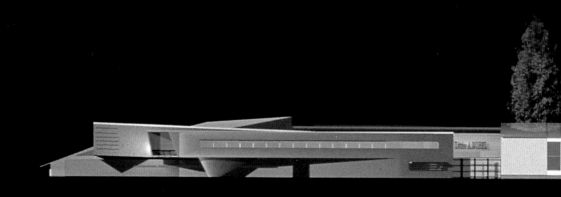

11

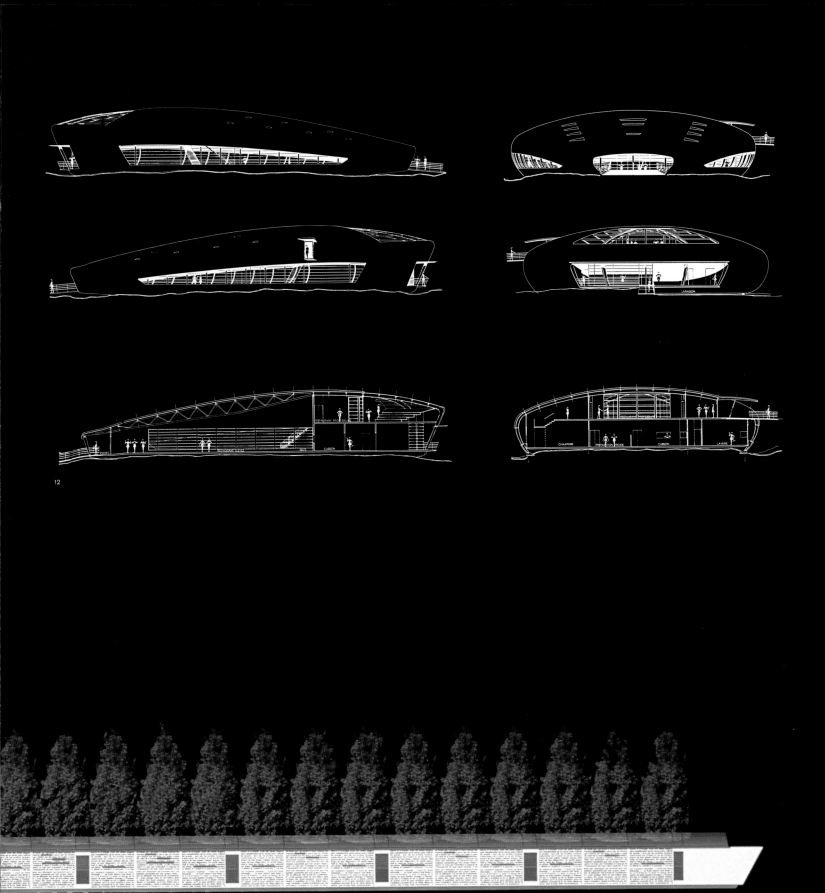

12

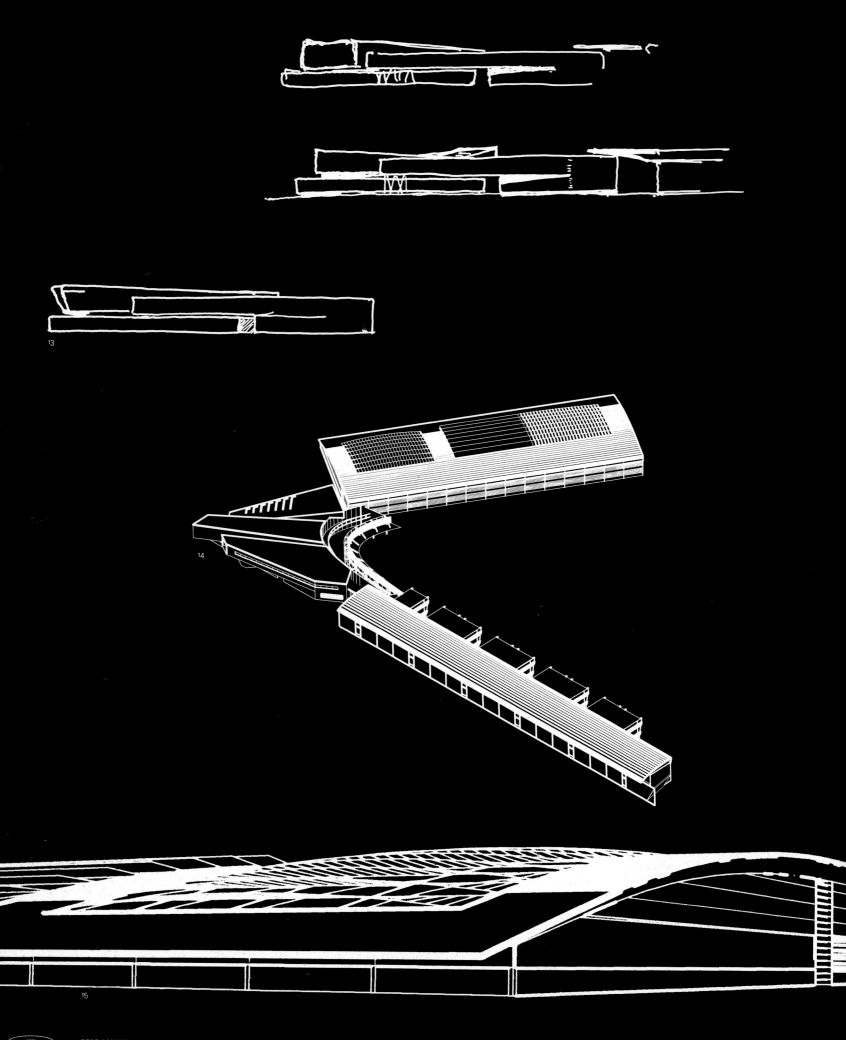

13

14

15

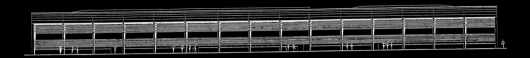

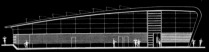

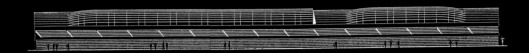

16

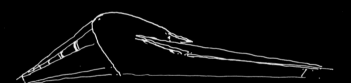

13 Sketch designs of the corner building.

14 Axonometric showing the formal relationship between the blocks .

15 Perspective of the workshop building showing its curved metal roof and junction with the new corner building.

16 Workshop building (clockwise from top): southwest, northeast and northwest elevations; cross section.

17 Axonometric showing the contrasting forms of the workshop block in the foreground and the classroom block behind.

17

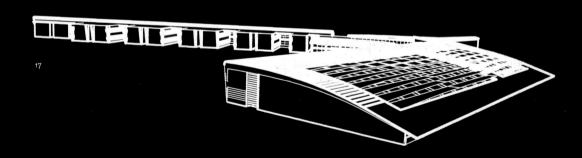

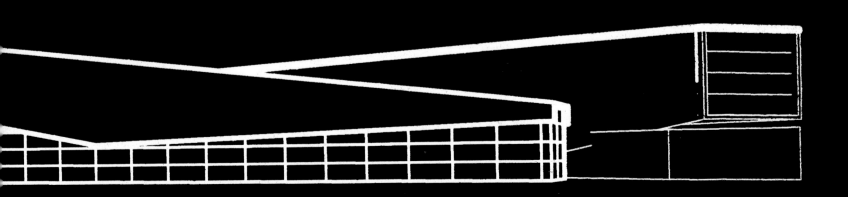

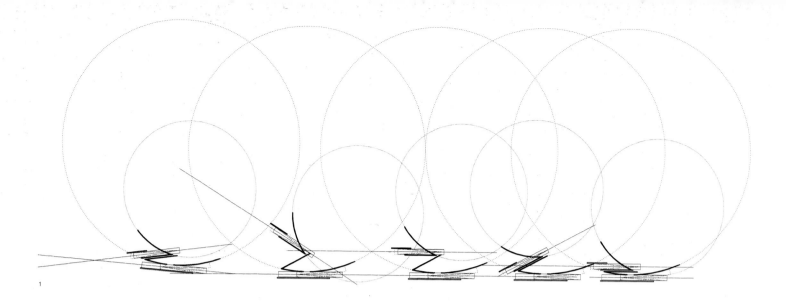

1

Hyper-Tension

Installation at the Centre National d'Art
Contemporain, Grenoble

1993

The exhibition, 'Application et Implication: modèle de pensée, acte de présence', at the Centre National d'Art Contemporain, Grenoble (an old factory where the parts for the Eiffel Tower were manufactured), was the first of a series in which young architects are invited to make an installation that expresses the ideas behind their work. Decq and Cornette's piece was a walk-through structure made of different materials that offered visitors a spatial experience intended to demonstrate the concepts of 'parcours'

and dynamic tension. The passage was enclosed by a curved screen on one side, and a straight one on the other, while a mirror reflected one's image back at oneself within the space.

The installation was designed to sum up the essential elements of an architecture generated by the ideal of constant movement, which for Decq and Cornette is the essential attribute of modernity. In the catalogue they explain: 'The variety of lines of escape (lignes de fuite) and perspective generates a permanent tension ... The parcours ... ensures a sequential perception of the space ... the threshold itself is extended, so that the boundary between interior and exterior becomes ambiguous.'

2

1 Diagram exploring the geometry generating the installation's design, and the development of the design process towards the final result (fig 6).
2 Conceptual model highlights the layout of the elements according to tensions generated by the juxtaposition of curved and straight lines.
3, 4 Study model viewed from both ends, showing the layering of

planes to contain space closely within the structure.
5 Axonometric clarifying the layering of elements and the tension between the curved and rectlinear geometries.
6 Model of the installation; the piece was designed to distil the essence of the architectural concepts and processes which inform Decq and Cornette's work.

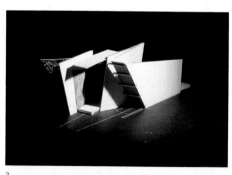

3

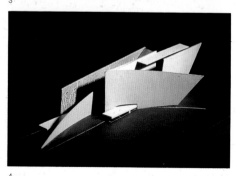

4

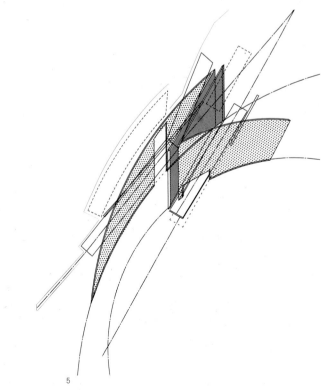

5

6

7, 8 Views of the installation in situ within the gallery space, creating its own spatial order within the massive volume of the old factory.

9 Detailed breakdown of the geometrical order governing the relationships between the elements.

10 Elevational view of the model.

11 Perspective view of the model.

12 Perspective view of the installation in situ.

7

8

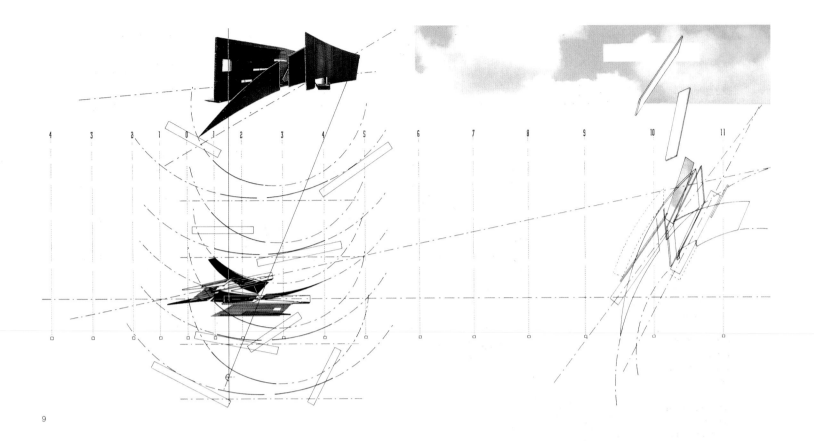

9

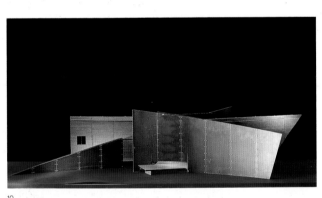

10

11

12

1 Mapping of the site with the main axes indicating the relationships between buildings.

2 View into the underground chamber of the pavilion, entered via a zig-zag ramp.

3 Side elevation of the Villa Zottmann showing the pointed prow of the glass showcase

containing the old facade, with new accommodation set at an angle behind.

4 Side elevation of the exhibition pavilion.

5 (overleaf) The belvedere is suspended over the edge of the cliff; a lightweight structure looking towards eastern Europe.

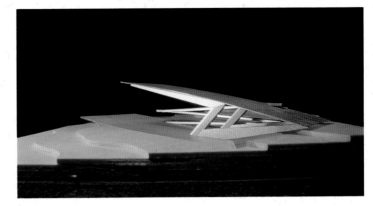

4

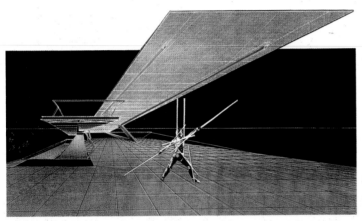

2

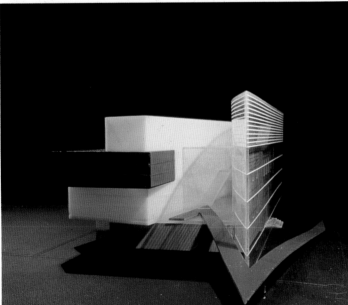

3

HIC SAXA LOQVVNTVR
Pfaffenberg Project, Vienna
1993

The Pfaffenberg project, an invited competition against Peter Cook and Christine Hawley (the winners), Ian Ritchie, Zaha Hadid and Maximiliano Fuksas, provided an opportunity to explore the ideas of dissociation and 'parcours' to the limit. The brief consisted of four separate elements – an open-air theatre, the renovation and conversion of the existing Villa Zottmann into a Roman archaeological museum, an exhibition pavilion, and a belvedere overlooking the river Danube – which had also to be linked together in some way to form a coherent entity.

The site is located on frontier territory on the Danube in Austria, a place of unsettled, even turbulent, history, both geological and political. The four elements of the programme are dispersed across the site: 'Four events, four epochs, developed like steps in a stair of time ... from the prehistoric to antiquity, from antiquity to the contemporary, from the contemporary to the future.'

The first element is the theatre, or Stone Grove, structured by the contour lines of a naturally occurring amphitheatre in the ground. It represents the memory of the prehistoric origins of the place, but also of an antique theatre from Greek civilization. The stage is a stone disc slipped into the land-mass, with storage underneath for technical equipment. Lit from below at night, it becomes a luminous surface. The seating is made out of metal beams set at different angles into the terraces. The stair is a clean incision into the contour lines, bordered by handrails made of glass panels embedded in the ground.

The Villa Zottmann museum represents the second epoch, antiquity. It houses Roman collections linked to Marcus Aurelius and the town of Carnuntum; but it also forms a link between antiquity and the present. The classical facade of the existing villa is lifted one metre above ground level, and enclosed in a glass showcase so that it acquires the status of an archaeological exhibit itself, with its foundations visible below through a glass floor like an excavation site. The space above the new ground level, behind the facade, is contained in three boxes stacked on top of one another. On the ground floor itself is the museum, encased in light-permeable stone bonded to glass, as if a sarcophagus; on the first floor is a library and offices, sheathed in lead, with a view towards the belvedere through moving panels; and on the top floor the reading room of the library, with access onto a terrace also orientated towards the belvedere.

The third element of the programme is the pavilion, which consists of an

5 (overleaf)

1

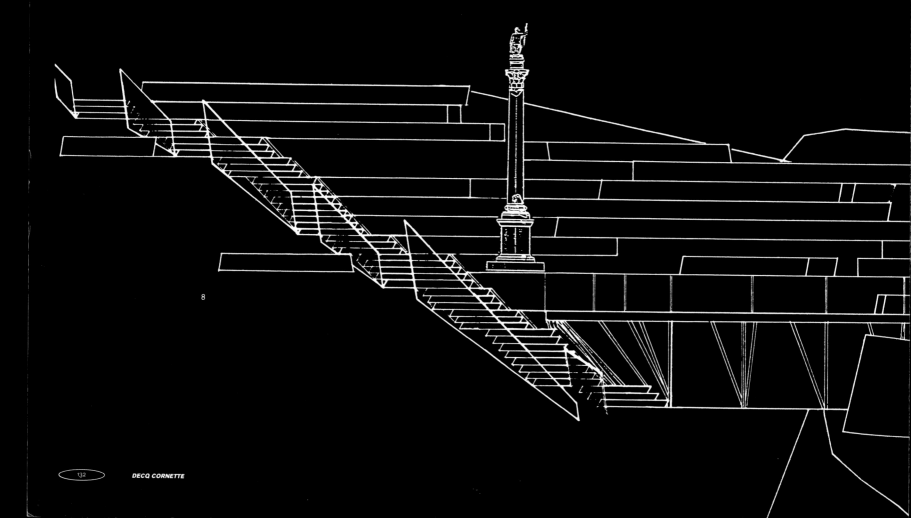

8

DECQ CORNETTE

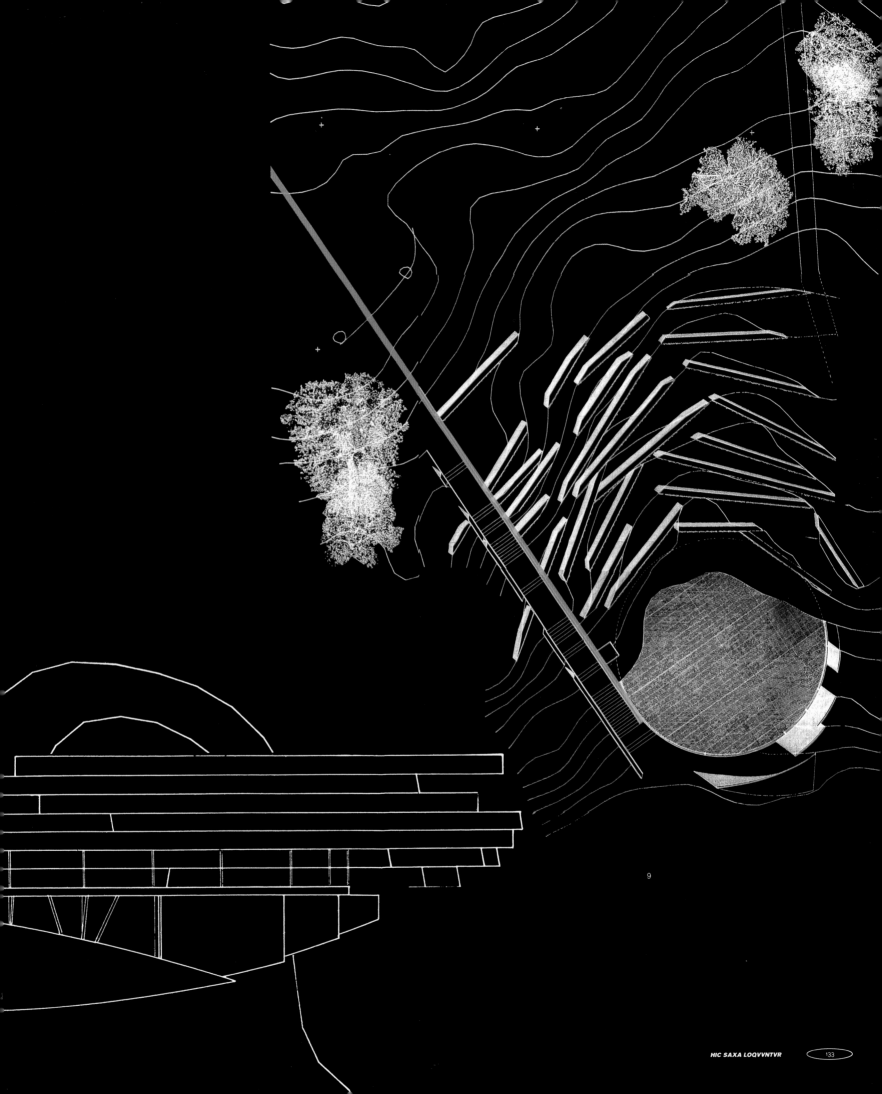

9

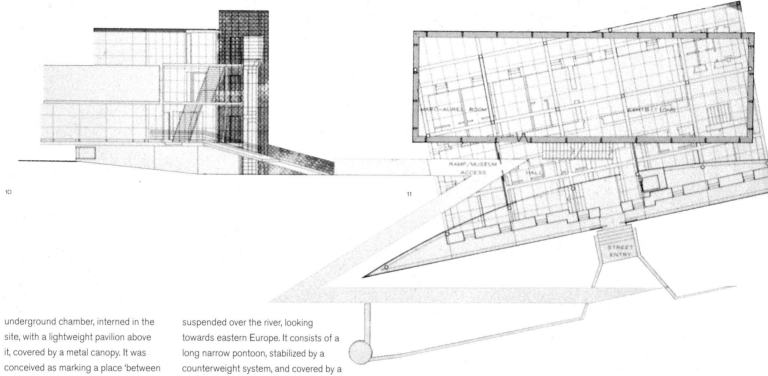

10

11

underground chamber, interned in the site, with a lightweight pavilion above it, covered by a metal canopy. It was conceived as marking a place 'between the earth and the sky'. The underground and above-ground elements are connected by a zig-zag ramp passing through a floor of stone bonded to glass which allows light to filter into the lower chamber. One of the walls of the lower chamber is made of glass, exposing a section of a geological reconstruction of the site, and thereby revealing the evidence of its archaeological makeup.

Finally, the belvedere is another lightweight construction located at a distance on the edge of the cliff, partly suspended over the river, looking towards eastern Europe. It consists of a long narrow pontoon, stabilized by a counterweight system, and covered by a canopy from which a two-way mirror is suspended over the water, pivoting in the wind. The belvedere simply perches on the edge of the site, detached from the ground itself. It represents the culmination of the progression through the space, extending from the Villa across the site to the boundary of western and eastern Europe, and beyond it, the future. It is 'at the same time the destination of the way and a point of suspension … the place of visual and virtual crossings of all boundaries'.

10 Section through the Villa Zottmann showing stacked boxes behind the front section comprising the classical facade enclosed in a glass showcase.
11 Plan of the Villa Zottmann showing the footprint of the new building superimposed over that of the original

at a height of 1m above ground level.
12 Section through the Villa Zottmann from the other side.
13 Rear elevation of the Villa Zottmann, with the glass front visible behind, and the roof terrace at second floor level looking out towards the belvedere.

14, 15, 16 Axonometrics of the Villa Zottmann from behind (fig 14), and from both sides. The contrasting volumes are clearly delineated, and their autonomy is emphasized by setting them at variable angles to each other.

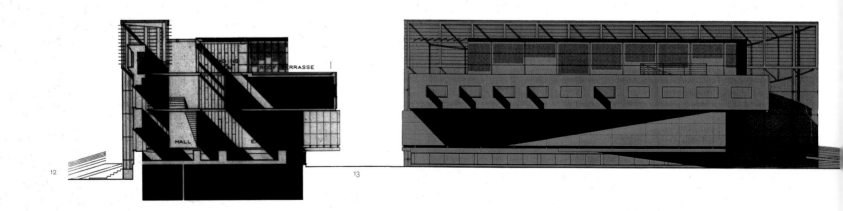

12

13

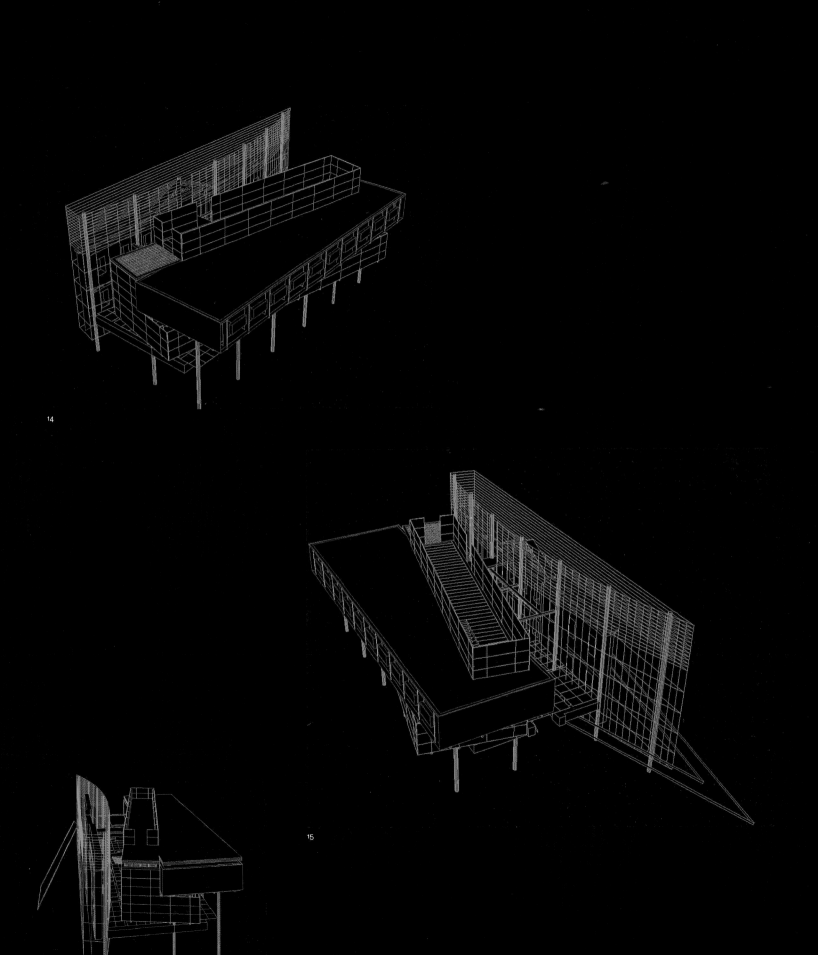

14

15

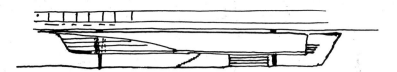

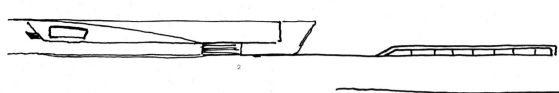

Motorway Viaduct and Operations Centre

Nanterrre

1993–96

'Our project is in the fullest sense a place of passage, infused with dynamic equilibrium. A single project, but seven transitions:
The transition towards Paris.
The transition from shadow into light.
The transition from weight to lightness.
The transition from static to dynamic.

The transition between north and south sections of the park.
The transition from the tunnel to the bridge.'

Decq and Cornette's poetic conception of a section of the motorway into Paris along the Grand Axe comprises the main route out of the heart of Paris along the Champs Elysées and through La Défense, marked by the Arc de Triomphe and the Grande Arche building located in a park underneath a viaduct. The viaduct forms a connection between

an underground tunnel passing under La Défense and a heavy concrete motorway bridge over the Seine and out of Paris through the suburb of Nanterre. The architects extended the scheme to embrace the redesign of the viaduct itself as a light metal structure supported on arc-shaped legs, or 'motor-footbridge' above the park. The road surface is designed in concrete, to create visual continuity with the existing bridge, but the structure as a whole, consisting of a series of clearly defined, detached

1 Long section through the building below and the viaduct above, with the operations room at centre and the look-out tower and mast antenna emerging above (top); cross section through the building and the viaduct (centre); elevation (below).

2 Sketches of the building's facade expressing the idea of speed and movement in the work.

3 View of underbelly of viaduct, with the building suspended underneath it. Hanging clear of the ground, it allows the park to be read as a continuous plane running through the site.

3

4

4 Cross section
through the
Administrative Centre,
operations room,
control room and
viaduct.
5 Side elevation of the
building and the viaduct
bridge, with glass
screens along either
side protecting drivers
from the glare and the
surrounding area from
traffic noise.
6 Section through the
edge of the viaduct
showing details of the
metal structure.

elements, is designed to produce an aerodynamic effect in contrast to the monolithic structure of the bridge. As the road emerges from the tunnel, and vice versa, it passes through a shell of glass screens, changing from opaque to translucent, which help to protect both the surrounding area from traffic noise, and drivers from the sudden glare experienced when emerging from a tunnel into the daylight. By night, these screens become luminous walls

reflecting light onto the road, and transforming this section of the Grand Axe into a shining ray visible from the ground below.

The building itself is, as it were, suspended from the underside of the viaduct, almost like a submarine structure lurking beneath the flow of vehicles on the surface. By detaching the building from the ground Decq and Cornette aimed to avoid creating a barrier across the park at the site of the viaduct, and

to preserve its physical and visual continuity: an open green space free from traffic, in which the motorway operations centre becomes a positive element integrated with the design and landscape vocabulary of the park.

The building contains two levels beneath the bridge, plus an underground level containing garaging, services and a covered patio and winter garden. On the ground floor is a police headquarters and public reception, with further

administrative accommodation on the upper floor, organized in a U-shaped plan around the operations room at the centre. This element emerges through the viaduct above road level as a look-out tower, crowned by a tall antenna and red light which indicates the nerve centre of the motorway operations system, and also provides a key landmark along the dramatic entrance sequence leading into the city.

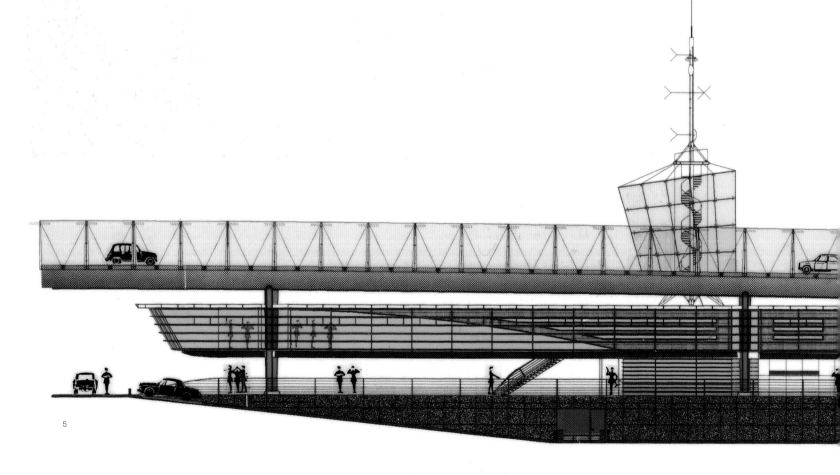

5

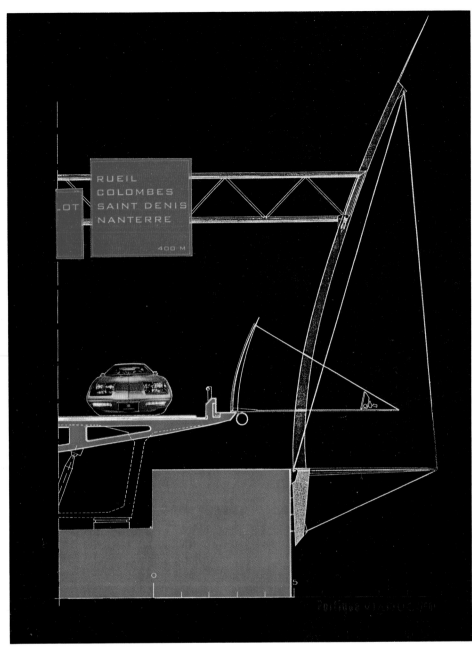

6

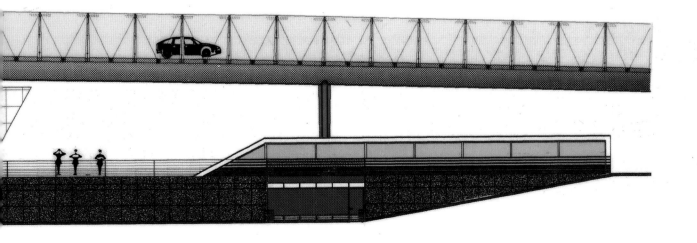

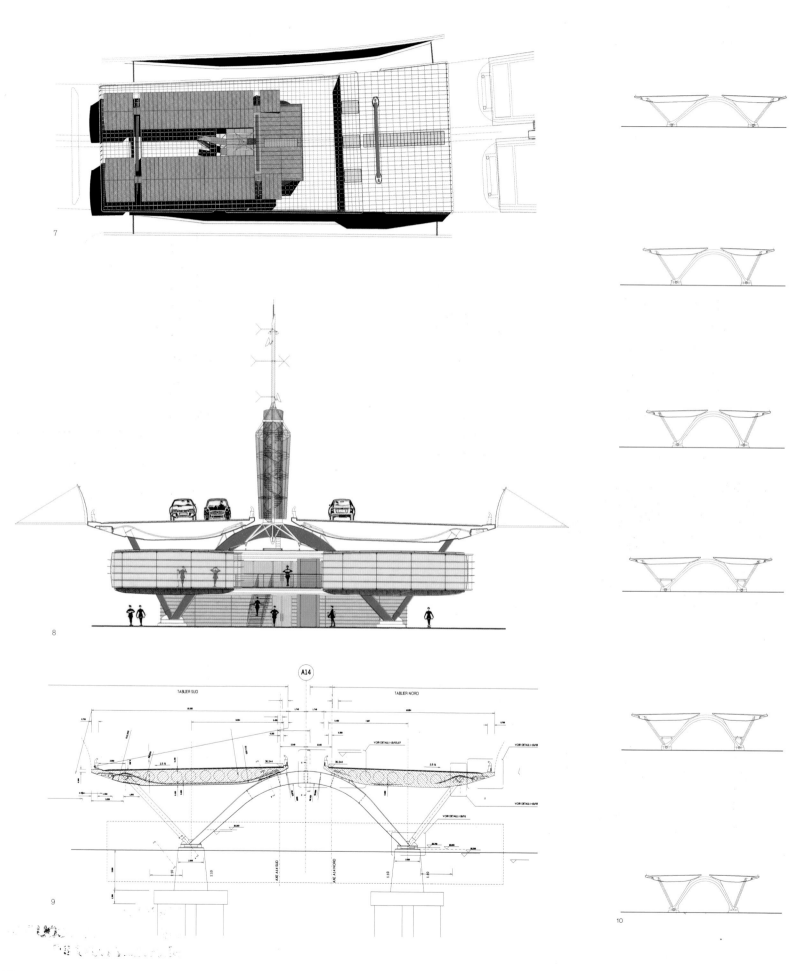

7

8

9

10

DECQ CORNETTE

7 Massing plan of the building under the viaduct.

8 Front elevation of the building, viewed beneath the viaduct.

9 Drawing of the metal structural system and concrete spans for the viaduct.

10 Sketch diagrams of structure exploring possible variations in the height of the viaduct.

11 Views of the viaduct under construction.

12 Elevation of the look-out tower and mast above road level, with a plan at the base of the structure.

11

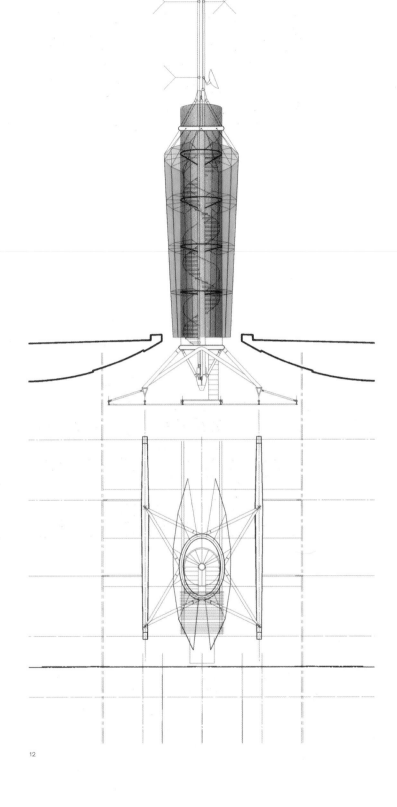

12

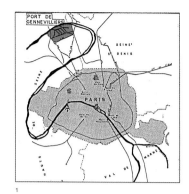

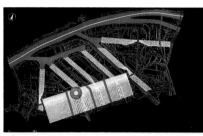

Port de Gennevilliers

Paris

1994–

The Port de Gennevilliers masterplan is based on the same process of mapping and site analysis as an earlier scheme for a new freight business park, Airlande, close to the airport outside Rennes. The town and port of Gennevilliers are located in the suburban hinterland of Paris at the new outer limit of the city's expansion, right on its main western development axis. Currently an industrial no-man's land, the port is to be given a new lease of life, to capitalize on the economic potential of its location. Its three main assets are its riverside aspect, its highly developed rail, road and water transport networks, and its position as a gateway in and out of Paris from the surrounding region stretching towards Le Havre.

Fundamental to Decq and Cornette's proposal for the revitalization of the port is the idea of linking it back into the town. Their strategy is again based on the concept of mapping existing infrastructure grids across the site, and using these patterns to structure a new layout, consisting of an 'active band', bordered by a zone of interface with the town on the south side, and a zone of interface with the river on the north side.

As in the Air and Space Museum scheme, the active band is treated as a linear node, or spine, running east–west through a new urban and industrial neighbourhood. It comprises an Esplanade du Port lined by banks, hotels, restaurants, bars, clubs and shops, with an arboretum on the south side and a pedestrian promenade on the north side. Beyond the Esplanade, the site is developed around the wet docks which penetrate it like the fingers of a glove, forming a series of canals. South of the esplanade these are extended in the form of green corridors connecting the port and the town.

The Port de Gennevilliers commission represents Decq and Cornette's first opportunity to play a significant role in developing new ground-rules for urban development in a specific area, albeit outside the immediate boundaries of the historic city.

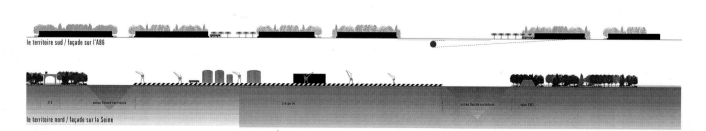

le territoire sud / façade sur l'A86

le territoire nord / façade sur la Seine

3

4

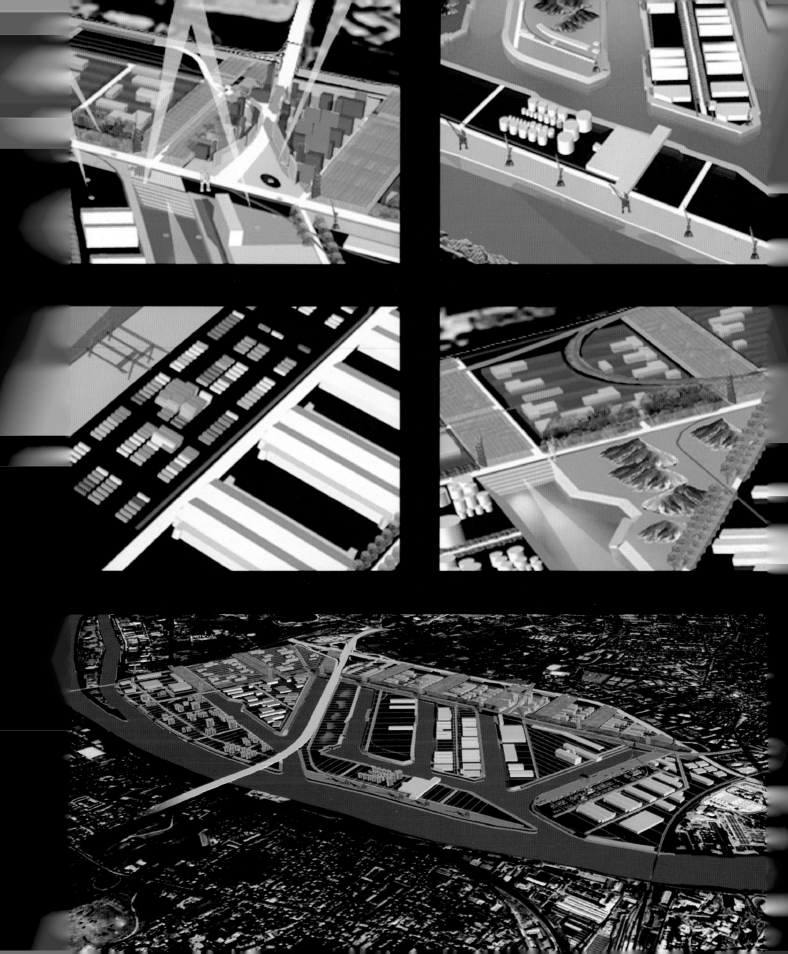

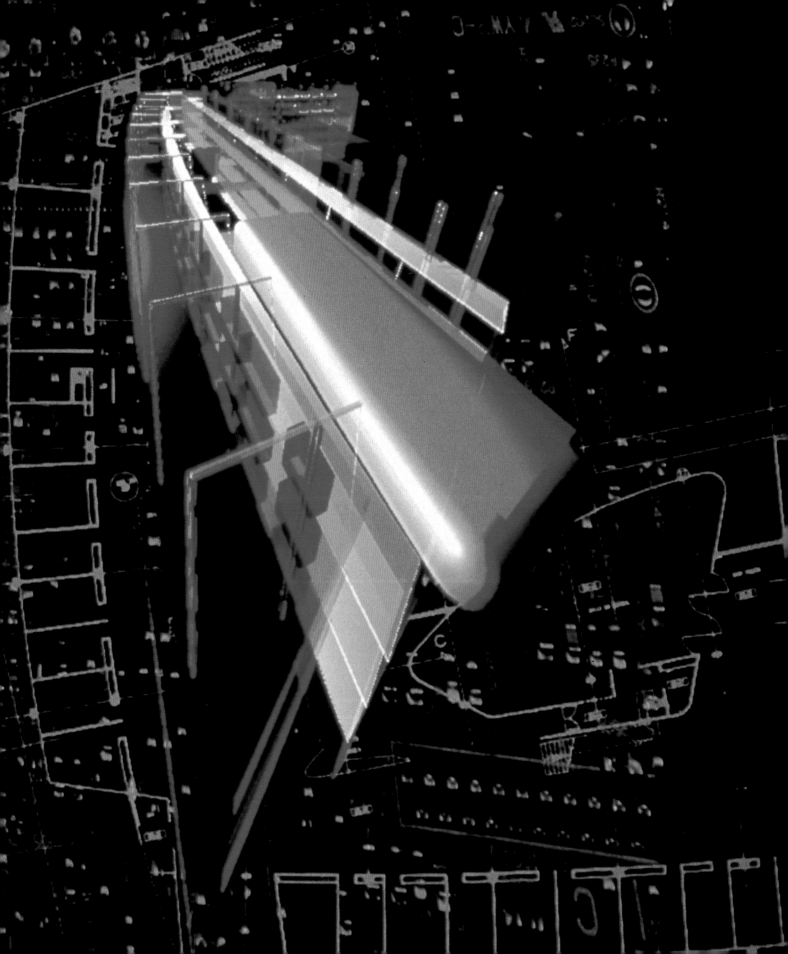

1 Computer-generated
image of the block
superimposed on the
plan of the building.
2, 3 Site and ground
plan showing floating
volumes containing the
public spaces.
4 Axonometric
showing the inverted
corner and outer

screens made of metal
louvres giving onto the
street. At roof level,
access to the terraces
along the perimeter of
the building is via two
footbridges across the
atrium roof from the
glazed clerestory
section of the building.

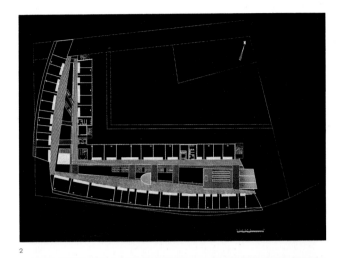

2

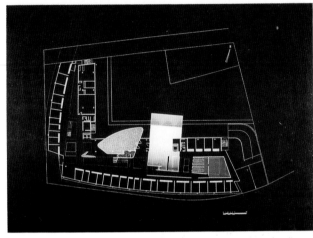

3

CNASEA – Centre National pour l'Aménagement des Structures des Exploitations Agricoles

Limoges

1994–

The image of the new CNASEA headquarters (a centre for the development of farming) is that of an 'hôtel particulier' in the town centre. It embodies an idea of modernity which is fused with a representation of institutional identity, at once open and closed. The exterior is designed to give a visual impression of a homogeneous, unified building addressing the town. However the internal spaces are divided into a series of vertical layers and, within that structure, broken down into two types – offices and communal public spaces – which are clearly dissociated from the other.

The public spaces are treated as floating volumes inserted into the centre of a vast atrium which forms the internal core of the building, running its entire length. These spaces, including the circulation routes around the sides of the atrium, function not only as interchanges and points of convergence which are crucial to the operation of the building, but also give real and symbolic expression to the company culture.

The south and west facades onto the street are constructed as a gently curved double layer representing a detachment of the physical and visual edges of the building. The transparent inner layer is of glass, while the outer layer consists of a screen made of horizontal metal louvres providing protection against the sun. This construction allows a clear view out of the building while giving privacy to the occupants, and creates a play of light and shadow across the facades of the building. On the north and east sides overlooking the garden, the facade consists of a single layer of glass.

As in the two school projects, the treatment of the urban corner was an important issue. The angle of the building is inverted, exposing the end walls of the two blocks where they would otherwise meet. Hence the corner opens up a new space on the edge of the street in which the entrance can be comfortably accommodated.

1

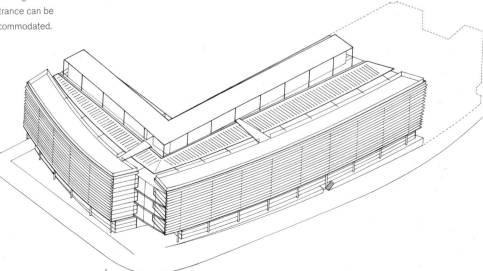

4

5

6

5 Computer-modelled
images of the building
showing floating internal
volumes and horizontal
circulation.
6 Long section
through the atrium of
the building showing
horizontal and vertical
circulation.
7 Long section and
axonometric views
showing the different
elements of the interior
space.
8, 9 Cross sections of
each wing, showing the
structure of the atrium
space, with layers of
gallery circulation along
either side and the stair
rising vertically through
the building.

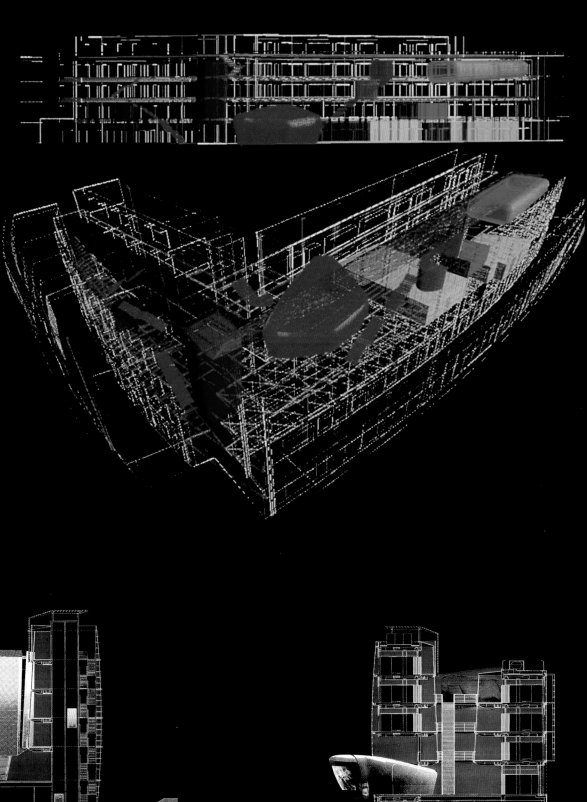

7

8

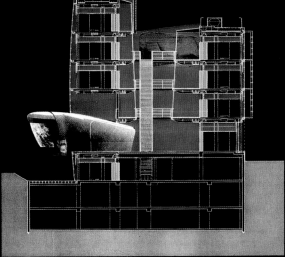

9

10 Aerial view of the scheme from the garden side.
11 Aerial view of the scheme from the end towards the corner, emphasizing the horizontal layering of the design.
12, 13 Perspective views of the stair.
14 A slice taken through an axonometric of the building, showing the composition of volume broken down into sections.
15 Computer-generated view through the main atrium space and up the stair.
16 Computer-generated detail of the stair suspended in space.

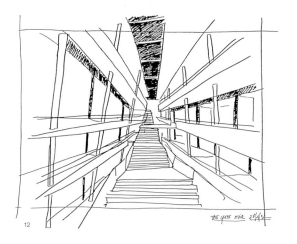

12

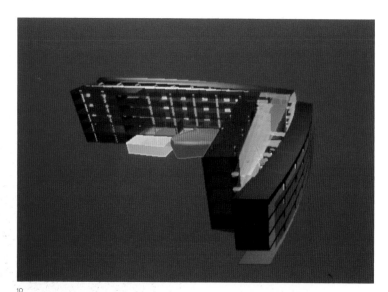

10

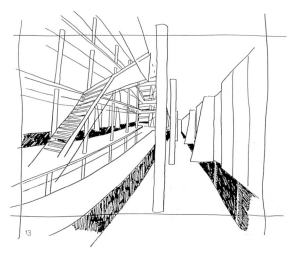

13

15

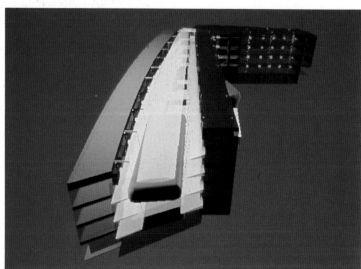

11

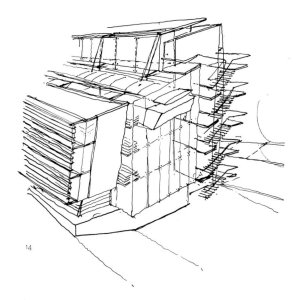

14

16

Awards

Winner,
Albums de la Jeune Architecture, Paris,
1986

Premier Award, Category C Winner, Ninth
International Prize for Architecture, London,
1990

Winner,
Prix Architecture et Lieux de Travail, Paris,
1990

Nomination,
Equerre d'Argent,
Paris, 1990

Winner,
Palmarès Départemental d'Architecture,
Rennes, 1991

Special Mention,
The Iritecna for Europe Award,
Milan, 1991

Finalist,
Premio Internazionale di Architettura
Andrea Palladio,
Vicenza, 1991

Winner,
Prix Plus Beaux Ouvrages de
Construction Métallique,
Paris, 1992

Winner,
Oscar du Design *Le Nouvel Economiste*,
Paris, 1992

Winner,
First prize, Category 1, 'Verre Feuillété'
Competition
Paris, 1993

Winner,
Benedictus Awards,
Washington, 1994

1984

August

Architecture Intérieure-crée (France), 'Au-
dessus de la Mayenne'

1986

February

Ouest France (France), 17 February 1986,
'Odile Decq: Lauréate Albums de la Jeune
Architecture'

October

Architectes – Architecture (France), No 171,
pp 26–27, 'Odile Decq, une femme qui sort
de la Mayenne'

November

Architectes – Architecture (France), No 172,
'Les Derniers premiers'

1988

October

Bulletin d'Informations Architecturales
(France), No 124, pp 1–3, 'Sous les toîts de
Paris' (Cinéma et Communication)

November

Architecture Intérieure-crée (France),
No 229, pp 148–149, 'Vol d'awacs sous
comble Haussmannien' (Cinéma et
Communication)

December

Architectes – Architecture (France), No 193,
p 30, 'Interview'

Le Moniteur (France), Special issue, p 152,
'Architecture 1988' (Cinéma
et Communication)

1989

September

Techniques & Architecture (France),
No 385, pp 102–103, 'Méthode des aperçus'

October

Techniques & Architecture (France),
No 386, p 14, 'Maquettes invraisemblables'
Pavillon de l'Arsenal (France), No 8,
p 8, 'Maquettes invraisemblables'

November

Le Moniteur (France), No 4486, pp 76–81,
'Un rideau de verre accroché à une fine
structure' (BPO)

December

D'Architectures (France), No 1, pp 32–36,
'VEC: le nec plus ultra?' (BPO)
Bouw Wereld (The Netherlands), No 25A,
pp 26–27, 'Banque Populaire – Brise-Soleil'
(BPO)
Le Moniteur (France), No 4488, p 105,
'Maquettes invraisemblables'
Paris Projet (France), No 27/28, p 195,
'L'aménagement de l'Est de Paris' (Social
Housing, Rue Manin, Paris)

1990

April

Topos (France), No 8, p 8, 'Clamart, crèche de l'Hôpital Béclère'

Bulletins d'Information Architecturales (France), No 139, pp 1–2, front cover, 'A Rennes, une usine pour banquiers' (BPO)

AMC – Le Moniteur (France), No 10, pp 45–52, 'Détails: façades de verre' (BPO)

Le Moniteur – Technologies 90 (France), Special issue, p 216, front cover, 'Des rideaux en verre vissé' (BPO)

May

D'Architectures (France), No 5, pp 12–15, front cover, 'Navire amiral à l'horizon' (BPO)

June

Sciences et Technologies (France), No 27/28, pp 23–25, 'Nouveaux matériaux, l'union fait la forme'

September

Communication Design – CB News (France), No 183, pp 22–23, '3 jeunes architectes inspirés' (BPO)

Building Design (GB), No 1004, pp 14–15, front cover, '9th international Prize for Architecture 1990' (BPO)

Magazine de la Construction (France), No 27, 'Actualité Architecture' (BPO)

Architecture Intérieure-crée (France), No 238, pp 130–137, front cover, 'Banque Populaire de l'Ouest' (BPO)

Techniques & Architecture (France), No 391, pp 108–111, 'Hérissé et poli'; pp 82–85, 'Le verre mis en oeuvre' (BPO)

City (France), No 63, p 56, 'Odile Decq, Archi-Destroy'

October

Trends (Belgium), p 164, '9ème Prix International d'Architecture BPO' (BPO)

Le Moniteur (France), '9ème Prix International d'Architecture BPO' (BPO)

November

Techniques & Architecture (France), No 392, p 77, 'Portrait de Groupe (Expo IFA)'

Architects' Journal (GB), p 18, 'Forty under 40'

Building Design (GB), No 1014, p 27, 'Two of a kind' (BPO)

AMC – Le Moniteur (France), No 16, p 20, 'French Perfection' (BPO)

Parcours (France), No 40, p 81, 'Cité en Exemple' (Apple Computer France Showroom)

D'Architectures (France), No 10, pp 16–19, front cover, 'Parcours – Duo bouillonnant' (BPO, Apple Computer France Showroom)

December

Libération (France), 22–23 December 1990, p 36, 'Le travail, quadrature de l'architecture' (BPO)

Le Moniteur (France), 'Prix Architecture et Lieux de Travail' (BPO)

Magazine de la Construction (France), No 30, p 16, '9ème Prix International de l'Architecture BPO' (BPO)

Archis (The Netherlands), p 20, '40 Architecten onder de 40'

Trends (Belgium), No 49, pp 138–141, 'Soft

Technologie' (BPO)

Techniques & Architecture (France), No 393, 'Bulletin AMO No 3 – Prix Architecture et Lieux de Travail' (BPO)

AMC – Le Moniteur (France), No 17, pp 143–203, 'Une année d'architecture 1900' (BPO)

D'Architectures (France), No 11, 'Industriels pour l'architecture' (BPO)

1991

January

Archi-crée (France), No 240, p 15, '9ème Prix International d'Architecture BPO' (BPO)

Architectural Design – The New Modern Aesthetic (GB), No 86, p 51–52; p 65–69, front cover, 'Recent Projects' (BPO, Maquettes Invraisemblables)

Bulletin de l'IFA (France), No 145, 'Prix Architecture & Lieux de Travail' (BPO, Apple Computer France Headquarters)

Techniques & Architecture (France), No 393, '9ème Prix International d'Architecture BPO' (BPO)

D'Architectures (France), No 12, p 16, 'Rétrospective 90' (BPO)

Magazine de la Construction (France), No 31, p 36, 'Lieux de travail, de la banque du troisième type…' (BPO)

February

CB News (France), Supplément Communication Design, No 198, p 3, 'Opinions'

Domino (Belgium), No 6, pp 52–54, front cover, 'Soft Technology' (BPO)

March

Archi-crée (France), No 241, pp 102–103, 'Apple Showroom – Nantes' (Apple Computer France Showroom, Cinéma et Communication)

April

Espace Bureau (France), No 8, pp 67–74, 'Rehabilitation' (Apple Computer France Showroom, Cinéma et Communication)

July

City (France), No 71, pp 60–65, 'L'invasion des néo-modernes' (BPO)

Techniques & Architecture (France), No 35, pp 144–146, 'Culture Technique – l'ascenseur: de la fonction à la séduction' (BPO, Téléservice, Créteil)

FP (Fusion Planning) (Japan), No 38, pp 13–17, 'Building Identity' (BPO)

August

Développeurs (France), Unnumbered issue, 'L'Architecture, Image d'Entreprise' (BPO)

Construction Moderne (France), No 68, pp 17–20, 'Les Materiaux Enjeux de la Construction'

September

Habitat Ufficio (Italy), No 51, p 3, pp 92–99, front cover, 'La banca a vela – a sailing bank' (BPO)

Techniques & Architecture (France), No 397,